JAMES II & VII
Britain's Last Catholic King

LAURA BRENNAN

PEN & SWORD
HISTORY

AN IMPRINT OF PEN & SWORD BOOKS LTD.
YORKSHIRE – PHILADELPHIA

First published in Great Britain in 2023 by
PEN AND SWORD HISTORY
An imprint of
Pen & Sword Books Ltd
Yorkshire – Philadelphia

Copyright © Laura Brennan, 2023

ISBN 978 1 39901 258 4

Typeset in Times New Roman 12/16 by
SJmagic DESIGN SERVICES, India.
Printed and bound in the UK by CPI Group (UK) Ltd.

Pen & Sword Books Limited incorporates the imprints of Atlas, Archaeology,
Aviation, Discovery, Family History, Fiction, History, Maritime, Military,
Military Classics, Politics, Select, Transport, True Crime, Air World, Frontline
Publishing, Leo Cooper, Remember When, Seaforth Publishing, The Praetorian
Press, Wharncliffe Local History, Wharncliffe Transport, Wharncliffe True Crime
and White Owl.

For a complete list of Pen & Sword titles please contact
PEN & SWORD BOOKS LIMITED
George House, Units 12 & 13, Beevor Street, Off Pontefract Road,
Barnsley, South Yorkshire, S71 1HN, England
E-mail: enquiries@pen-and-sword.co.uk
Website: www.pen-and-sword.co.uk

Or

PEN AND SWORD BOOKS
1950 Lawrence Rd, Havertown, PA 19083, USA
E-mail: Uspen-and-sword@casematepublishers.com
Website: www.penandswordbooks.com

Contents

Acknowledgements

Once again I find myself getting to know a historical figure and challenging myself to find out more about them in order to understand what motivated them to behave as they did during their lifetime. History can sometimes paint historical figures in certain lights and I like to explore whether the reputations, be they good or bad, are justified. This book was meant to help me get through the pandemic and lockdowns of 2020/21, it has instead become learning curve that taught me things about myself, as well as James II, during the process of writing. I am beyond grateful to Jonathan Wright and the team at Pen & Sword as well as the lovely Kate Bohdanowicz, for giving me the opportunity to write this book and challenge myself, once again. I would also like to thank my assigned editor Karyn Burnham – a good editor allows an author's work to shine.

Special thanks needs to go to my brother, Mark Linehan, who is my cheerleader and is always optimistic and encouraging. My uncles Paul Brennan and Peter Bradley, again for their encouragement and faith in me, as well as the lunches, wine and chocolate – vital essentials for finishing a book. To my best friend Ruth Sullivan, thank you for the dog memes, for making me chuckle and being there when I needed a friend. To my other bestie Julia Hopkins, who even from the other side of the globe and in a different time zone, encouraged and supported me during these very strange few years and the process of this third book. Thanks also goes to Dr Sean Lang, who without realising it, acted as my personal conscience, forcing me to re-examining my preformed opinions of James, especially when reading back my drafts. Your role as Jiminy Cricket made me look for the good when James was at his most frustrating! To Haley Foster, your kind words and history memes have always come at the right time. To Rob Leadbeater, thank you as always darling, we must toast James II very soon!

Honourable mentions should go to Professor John Miller who supervised me during my dissertation on the Duke of Monmouth and it was during the research for that part of my MA that I encountered James II & VII for the first time.

Lastly thank you to anyone who had brought, read, borrowed, reviewed and recommended any of my books including this one. Without an audience curious to know what I have to say, I could not do this and fulfil my dream of being a published author for a third time. I am always touched by your kind words and support.

Laura Brennan, May 2022

Introduction

It is vital as a historian to look at all your subjects objectively; however, this is easier with some historical figures than others and in the case of James II & VII, that could at times, be a bit of a challenge. Throughout this book, I have, I hope, remained unbiased and fair in my assessment of him as both a man and a king. Through the process of writing this book, I have been pleasantly surprised that my previous opinions towards the last Catholic monarch of England and Britain have shifted. This happened largely through examining his life before he unexpectedly took the throne. This subsequently made it easier to understand why he behaved as he did and my empathy towards him mainly as human rather than a monarch has grown. At times, my frustration with him has also grown because James was unable to learn from his errors nor see the strength of his position or circumstances and utilize them fully.

A book of this length is not intended to be an in-depth biography, but is designed hopefully to be approachable and easy to access for all readers, so that they too can examine the last Stuart king, who was also the UKs last Catholic monarch and father to two Stuart queens.

The first part of the book deals with James Stuart's life while he was the Duke of York. To say that he had an interesting and eventful childhood and adolescence is rather an understatement. By his early adulthood he was an exile, had lost his father to the executioner, witnessed Civil War battles first hand, been held as a hostage during the Civil Wars and had to live in the shadow of an older brother. This is enough to explain some of the personality traits that James the man and James the king developed, as well as why his life took the twists and turns it did.

James would grow, gain in confidence and evolve during the Restoration court of his brother. He also faced personal and political opposition due to his Catholic conversion. This hostility increased when it became obvious that Charles II would not have a legitimate male heir. During this time as the Duke of York, we glimpse aspects of his personality and character that would shape the monarch he became in February 1685.

At first glance it may seem that the first part of the book, which does not deal with his reign, is top heavy, but given the arguments I make and the length of his reign it was important to the book and the points I am making.

Although his time upon the thrones of England, Scotland and Ireland was brief, it was no less eventful. And even after he abandons his crown and responsibilities in December 1688, his actions and subsequent attempts to get the thrones back have had a lasting impact upon the political and social history of Britain, and particularly Ireland, making him an important historical figure often overlooked due to his perceived failures and faith, rather than the consequences of his actions and their legacy.

It is important to state that I am not a specialist in military history. Where I have looked at and described battles and sieges, it is because it was relevant to explaining James and his actions and I have aimed to make these events easy for the general reader, who may not have a background in military history, to read and understand. Within the bibliography there are more military-focused materials listed should you want a more technical and in-depth look at this part of James's life.

In more recent years, historians have revised the use of the term 'English Civil War' to describe the series of wars that started in Ireland, spread to Scotland and lastly was fought in England, between 1642 and 1651. These events led up to King Charles I, losing his head on the scaffold in 1649. These events also led to his son, Charles II, to attempt to reclaim his father's lost the throne of Scotland, in order to try and regain England and Ireland too. The more modern and accurate term favoured today by historians for this period is 'The Wars of the Three Kingdoms', and I also choose to use this term.

However I did choose to use the term 'Glorious Revolution' to describe the events that took place at the end of 1688, when James lost his thrones, but I acknowledge that this term is viewed as problematic. Upon balance, I felt it was the most appropriate term to use in this instance, as well as being the most commonly used and understood name for these important events in James's story.

From the reign of James I & VI the monarchies of England and Scotland became joined so I have used the term United Kingdom throughout the book for ease of understanding for the reader although legally all the nations were not joined until during the reign of James's daughter, Queen Anne, in 1707 under the Act of Union.

When it has come to dates, I have endeavoured to use, to the best of my knowledge, the Julian calendar because the change to the Gregorian calendar did not happen in England and Ireland until 1752. So for the sake of simplicity (and my sanity) I decided not to use dual dating showing 'old' and 'new' dates as some primary and secondary sources of the period do. There is an eleven-day difference between European dates and British dates for the period, so you may find different dates stated in other books and sources. This is especially true if the book is written using European sources and from a European perspective, rather than a British view point. Any error in this is mine and I have double checked all dates.

When it came to writing about the events of the Williamite War (1689–91) and the use of the name for the city of Derry/Londonderry, I choose to use the Irish 'Derry' rather than the British 'Londonderry'. This felt more in tone and style of the theme and topic of the book and the chapter. The use of Derry is in no way a reflection of my personal politics or opinions towards the region.

Saint-Germain-en-Laye, the last home of James II and his wife Mary of Modena, was located seventeen miles from central Paris. I will frequently shorten it to St Germain within the text and this refers to the chateau and its surrounding small town, rather than the central arrondissement, of the same name within central Paris.

Due to the number of Marys in James's life, I will refer to Mary II (Williams III's wife and James's daughter) as Mary, while giving his second wife her full anglicised name of Mary of Modena, in order to easily distinguish between them.

Through personal preference I have used the 24-hour clock because this is easier to distinguish day versus night and often when time is specified it relates to military engagements, so it feels more logical.

I hope you find my appraisal of one of our less known, yet constitutionally important monarchs of history, both insightful and thought provoking.

PART 1

The
Duke of York
1633–1685

The Inherited Misfortune of the House of Stuart

To understand how James was shaped, it is important to look at the history of his family both before and after they took the English throne. Even if you know very little about Scottish history it is well known that many consider the royal house of Stewart 'cursed'. At the very least they were an unfortunate royal family. The spelling of Stewart is changed to Stuart upon the James VI taking the English throne and he became James I of England upon Elizabeth I's death, in March 1603. This series of unfortunate Stewart monarchs started with James I of Scotland, who was assassinated in 1437, being stabbed sixteen times; during the attack he tried to escape down a sewer.

James II of Scotland (not our James) gained the throne at 6 years of age and would become a thug. He decided to meddle in the affairs of the English during the Wars of the Roses, and died a rather unpleasant death while getting too close to a state-of-the-art fifteenth-century cannon. The cannon exploded next to him and ripped off one of his legs at the thigh. He inevitably died of his injuries. He was succeeded by his son, James III; he was unpopular because he sought an alliance with the 'auld enemy', England. His son (yet another James!) was the figurehead of a rebellion against his father, defeating him at the Battle of Sauchieburn; James III was killed not long after, and James IV would regret his involvement in his father's downfall.

Unlike the three James's before him, James IV had a relatively successful first part of his reign, until he too, decided to mess about in English affairs. Slyly, while Henry VIII was away in France, James IV invaded England. Henry had left his first wife, Catherine of Aragon, in charge. Catherine was a child of war, she was the daughter of Ferdinand

and Isabella of Spain who defeated the Muslims within southern Spain. James IV had greatly underestimated this warrior queen. His invasion ended in the infamous Battle of Flodden in September 1513. James IV died on the battlefield; his body had sustained heavy injuries and multiple wounds. Catherine informed her husband in France of her victory over the Scottish by sending him James's bloody and torn coat, as well as part of his armour from the battle – how romantic.

His son, James V, would also suffer the might and wrath of Henry VIII. James V's mother was Henry VIII's sister, Margaret Tudor. This made Henry, James V's maternal uncle. Henry requested that his nephew cut ties with the church in Rome and start a Scottish Reformation. James declined his uncle's request and the climax of their disagreement resulted in the Battle of Solway Moss (1542) in which the Scots were defeated. Tragically, James V never recovered mentally from this defeat at the hands of Henry VIII. It is said that he literally gave up the will to live, leaving the throne of Scotland to his 6-day-old daughter, Mary (Queen of Scots).

Of all the Stewarts, Mary is the most romanticised. She was the queen of Scotland from six days old; Dauphine of France from five years old; Queen of France (1559–60); widowed twice (King François I, King of France, in 1560 and Henry Stuart, Lord Darnley, in 1567); surrounded by scandal and accused of killing her second husband, weeks later she married the Earl of Bothwell – a rogue of the first order and the man who most likely killed her previous husband. She was then forced to abdicate by her half-brother in favour of her infant son, had to flee imprisonment from Scotland, and then spent the last nineteen years of her life under house arrest in Elizabeth I's England. While under house arrest, Mary got herself embroiled in several plots to overthrow Elizabeth so that eventually, Elizabeth was left with no choice but to sign Mary's death warrant. Between all her adventures, Mary did manage to have a son, James, with her second husband Lord Darnley, who would eventually inherit the English throne from Elizabeth I in 1603, becoming James I of England and VI of Scotland.

James I of England and VI of Scotland seemed to be the exception to the Stuart curse. He had been a king since infancy, and although he had lost his mother to the executioner, he had been estranged from her since he was an infant. Little changed when James VI arrived in England from Scotland. He was a more relaxed king, informal in dress and speech than Elizabeth had been, or his son Charles would be after him. He was Protestant in faith, an attribute that nearly caused him to be blown up in the Gunpowder Plot of 1605 by radical Catholic extremists. However, having survived that through the discovery of the plot, James I brought a stability with him to England. This feeling of political stability, that had been lacking through Elizabeth's reign, was firstly due James being male. Although Elizabeth had ruled with 'a heart and stomach of a King', she had ultimately been a woman. Her reign had been made more unstable because she choose not to marry and ruled independently. Politically and constitutionally this was unsettling, particularly later in her reign. The other big factor was the fact that Pope Pius V had issued a Papal Bull excommunicating Elizabeth and encouraging Catholics, both English and international, to dethrone her. This increased tensions between Catholics and Protestants in England, as well as affecting politics both at home and internationally. James was married and had an established heir in the form of Prince Henry, and had even produced 'spares', primarily in Prince Charles, but also in Princess Elizabeth. Regardless of his rumoured homosexual tastes, James had done his royal duty and procreated. The English felt secure and happy enough for him to take the English throne, despite being from the land of the auld enemy – Scotland. when King James I arrived from Scotland therefore, he brought with him a more traditional, cohesive, male and stable monarchy to the English throne.

Unfortunately, despite moving south of the border, and seemly skipping a generation, the 'curse' of the house of Stuart did not stop. In 1612, Henry, the Prince of Wales – who was shaping up to be everything a king of Britain and Ireland should be – became seriously ill and within four weeks he was dead. Henry had been Protestant, hale, hearty, athletic, handsome, charming and well liked and described as 'robust in health'. He apparently enjoyed swimming in the River Thames daily. Unfortunately, this may well be the possible cause of his decline and eventual premature death. The 18-year-old became ill and exhausted choosing, uncharacteristically, to stay in bed. Then followed a fever, a general feeling of being unwell before developing into terrible problems within his digestive system, primarily his intestines. Today, better knowledge of waterborne illnesses, hygiene practices, sewers and vaccines help keep people safe from bacteria and viruses such as typhoid. Poor Prince Henry was less lucky, finally dying on 16 November 1612. James I was heartbroken at the loss of his eldest son, and England never got a King Henry IX.

The fate of the country now would be in the hands of Prince Charles, who was the sickly weak royal child; he was the opposite of what Henry had been. During childhood, Prince Charles had suffered from rickets and had developed a nervous speech impediment. The state of Prince Charles's health worried James I's government at the time of Henry's death. They were so concerned that they seriously considered that the throne should pass to James's daughter, Princess Elizabeth, instead of Prince Charles. Their fears would be unfounded, and given time to grow and develop, Charles blossomed into a highly cultured man, who was a competent horseman and confident fencer; his childhood rickets did not impact him physically as a man. It was as a young, cultured and impressionable prince that Charles would find inspiration on how to be a monarch, while visiting the Spanish Habsburg court in search of a bride.

The bride that had come to Prince Charles's attention was Spanish Infanta of the ruling Habsburgs, Maria Anna. Although she belonged to the most powerful ruling family on continental Europe, there was one small problem: Maria Anna was deeply Catholic, which of course caused concern within the governing Anglican establishment back home in England. Although still only the heir to the throne, Charles found himself facing these concerns in the House of Commons while his father was indulging in that most Stuart of pastimes, horse racing at Newmarket – a habit his grandsons Charles II and James II both enjoyed.

As the House of Commons debated and argued over his potential choice of bride we see for the first time anger and frustration from Charles. His father's government was debating what he felt should be a private and personal matter. And here lies the problem with Charles I and later on in his son, James II. They both failed to grasp that in their position as monarch, there was no such thing as a 'private life', and that they needed to comply with social expectations and be completely transparent – including when their queens gave birth. In what is an intimate, private and personal time, the queen was expected to deliver her child with the court at very close quarters. This would become even less private after the Warming Pan Scandal of 1688 at the birth of James's son, Prince James Francis Edward Stuart, when the queen and her ladies were accused of exchanging a dead child for a live baby boy by smuggling the supposed changeling into the birthing room in a bed warming pan. The political fallout of this accusation and the role it played in James II's fate is explored later in the book. Royals were allowed no privacy or choice in other areas of life too; how they choose to pray for example, and who they should marry for the good of international politics and alliances. How a monarch lived his life at this time affected the nations they ruled politically, socially and religiously, especially in a post-Reformation and counter Reformation period such as the seventeenth century.

Of course the more that parliament debated the issue, the stronger Charles's opposition and resentment grew and the more he wanted to pursue this possible union with the Catholic Infanta. This was not just personal for Charles, this was an opportunity for him to prove himself to other European powers, to parliament and even to his father the king. In February 1623, Charles took matters into his own hands and travelled uninvited and without warning to Madrid, in a quest to try to woo his bride and broker the marriage terms with the powerful Habsburg court of Philipe IV.

During his stay in Spain, the young impressionable Charles saw how a very Catholic court, with an absolute monarch, ruled and was in control. In Spain, there was no argumentative and difficult parliament debating the personal life of the Infanta, in Spain this was a family issue. This must have seemed so liberating to Charles after having dealt with parliament for his father over the issue of his own marriage.

Due to the fact Spain was (and still is) a conservative Catholic country, the Pope was brought into the diplomatic negotiations for the potential marriage between Spain and England. When Charles heard the terms tabled by the Pope and the Spanish, he must have known that any hopes of being able to marry Maria Anna were gone. The Pope and Spain wanted all of the anti-Catholic laws within Britain to be legally dissolved and for Catholics to be free to worship in the open without fear of prosecution. To ensure that these terms were fully met, and not just in England, but all of Britain, the Infanta would remain in Spain for a full year after their marriage for the terms of the negotiation to be implemented. Poor Charles, he must have been very disappointed.

Both the background history of the House of the Stuart in Scotland and what Charles witnessed while in Spain would be reflected, directly or indirectly, in his feelings towards parliament later when he inherited the throne. These opinions and feelings would then be inherited and subsequently parroted by his equally frustrated second son, James, when he became a king. The consequences of these feelings, actions and their behaviours would lose them both their power and their position.

Although Charles's eventual wife, Henrietta Maria, was both staunchly Catholic and also French, she was a far better diplomatic choice for a bride than the Spanish Infanta. As Charles I was the royal 'spare', and should not have been king, it is easy to understand why, after the birth of his own son Prince Charles (later Charles II), it was important for him to also have a 'spare' in the royal nursery. The couple welcomed a second son, James, Duke of York, on 14 October 1633 at the royal palace of St James in London.

They named their second son, after his paternal grandfather, James I of England and VI of Scotland. Little Prince James was given his formal titles upon his baptism on 24 November 1633. His official titles linked him to England, with the dukedom of York, while the dukedom of Albany would be his link to the ancestral homeland of the house of Stuart, Scotland. The service was carried out by the Protestant Archbishop of Canterbury, William Laud, within the private chapel of St James's Palace in London. The prince's godparents were Elizabeth, Queen of Bohemia; her son, Charles Louis, who also happened to be the infant Prince's cousin, and Fredrick Henry, Prince of Orange. All of the godparents were of the Protestant faith and all sent representatives to stand in proxy for them during the actual baptism ceremony. Even from his birth, the future of James, Duke of York, future had been linked to the Dutch House of Orange and the Protestant Dutch Republic.

The young Duke of York would join the household of his elder brother Charles, Prince of Wales, which was located at Richmond Palace, in Surrey. The royal siblings were joined by the orphaned Duke of Buckingham George Villiers, and his younger brother Francis Villiers. Unlike his brother Charles, James did not form a close friendship with his childhood resident playmates. This is reflected in James's interaction with Buckingham later during the years of Charles's reign, after the Restoration.

The young Duke of York was encouraged to make a career for himself in the military rather than the church (although as we see later in the book, he may well have been a happier man if he had been allowed to go into the church). He was bestowed the title of Lord High Admiral in 1638 when he wasn't yet 5 years old. Not only did this opportunity give the royal spare a path to follow when he came of age, but it would mean that those who undertook the duties of position in the meantime were given the opportunity to be of service to the monarch, but it limited their power as the position already had a successor.

Like many royal children, the princes were brought up away from their parents. Both were well provided for; among the activities enjoyed by the young Duke of York, Prince of Wales and the Buckingham boys were dancing, archery and fencing. Historian John Callow describes the Duke of York's education as being 'taught to write legibly and could spell adequately enough' (*The Making of King James II – The Formative Years of a Fallen King* J. Callow p.34). Although formal education in his childhood was patchy, the Duke of York was an intelligent man. Later we will see that during his final exile in France, he compiled a (now lost) memoir of his life – such an achievement requires a certain level of intelligence – and he was an avid reader.

Having looked at the childhood experiences of both royal brothers, nothing in James's upbringing stands out to make him a very different king to his more successful brother Charles. The Duke of York's difference in personality seems to stem from natural sibling rivalry that in this case is exaggerated due to them being royal male siblings. It is fair to say that he inherited his father's stubbornness and belief in the divine right of kings – maybe that is because they were both 'spares', that became kings. Children who lose a parent young, and in such circumstances as the royal princes, often have rose-tinted memories of that deceased parent, and James seems to have had a more romanticised memory of his father than did his brother Charles. The little Duke of York was only 8 when the king and his parliament entered into the first of the Civil Wars. These over romanticised images of his father would have been reinforced by his mother, the dowager queen, Henrietta Maria who worshipped her dead husband.

When looking at the history of the Stuarts and what James was born into, it makes it easier to understand the attitudes, thoughts and character of the later James II – both the man and the king. It give perspective to the social, religious and political aspects of the reign of Charles I and how it influenced his younger son as a man as well as a Stuart king.

The Civil Wars of the Three Kingdoms

The events of the reign of James I are important for a fuller understanding of how the seventeenth century's religious and political tensions started in the Stuart reigns. The civil conflicts of the Wars of the Three Kingdoms would eventually bring about the start of political modernisation and begin to revolutionise the role of the monarchy of Britain. This was not before much blood was spilt within Scotland, Ireland and England, and the fall of Charles I. More commonly and inaccurately known as the English Civil Wars, The Wars of the Three Kingdoms are also invaluable in understanding the attitudes, motivations, politics, and causes of fear that would emerge during the crisis point of King James II's reign in late 1688. These events also help explain why James would lose his thrones.

The House of Tudor came to an end with the death of Elizabeth I in the spring of 1603; the new ruling house of the Stuarts heralded the beginning of one of the most turbulent periods in British history – not just to their new home of England, but to the whole of the British Isles and Ireland. Both James I and then his son Charles interrupted the principle of the divine right of kings in very different styles during their respective reigns. So much so that their contrasting styles created fear among the peoples of Scotland, Ireland and England, which brought about a series of wars leading to an explosive climax consisting of a mix of fear about politics and of religious dogma. These fears had been simmering socially and politically since the European Reformation begun by Martin Luther in 1517, the subsequent English Reformation under Henry VIII in 1533, then latterly the Scottish Reformation started by fiery preacher John Knox in 1547.

The first big event in the British reign of the Stuarts after 1603 clearly demonstrates this social, religious and political cocktail of fear – and would later add to fears in Britain in 1685 when James II acceded to the throne as a Catholic. The event was the discovery of the Gunpowder plot, on 5 November 1605.

The plot was devised by a group of Jesuit radical Catholics who wanted to blow up the Houses of Parliament at the state opening of parliament, in the hope of killing the Protestant James I, his heir, and the sitting members of parliament and Lords of the realm all at the same time. Although the plot was devised by Robert Catesby, there were eleven members of the group, all of whom were caught and arrested. The most famous of these was Guy Fawkes, who is remembered because he was arrested at the scene of the crime. Subsequently, all the plotters were tortured, found guilty of high treason and executed for their crimes.

By 1688, feelings of fear towards Catholics by the Protestant majority would be felt again after almost four years under the reign of Catholic James II. They had begun see that he was embodying the autocratic tendencies associated with a Catholic monarch and feared he would achieve his pro-Catholic agenda of reconverting his kingdoms to Catholicism and ruling in an dictatorial style.

When James II's father, Charles I, inherited the throne in 1625, the kingdoms of England, Scotland and Ireland each had a very different religious make up. It was Charles's desire to unit his kingdoms under not just one monarch, but one religious doctrine, that would become his personal crusade and become the spark that started the civil conflicts which would eventually lead him to the executioners block in January 1649.

In 1625, England was primarily Anglican Protestant. There were Catholics, mostly situated in the north of England, but there was also a growing number of non-Reformist Protestants who felt that the English church was not Protestant enough. This group were known as Puritans. In Scotland, the Reformation was far more in line with the Protestants of northern Europe compared to their neighbours south of the boarder. The Scottish church, known as the kirk, had no hierarchy, unlike both the Church of England who had the monarch as their leader, or the Catholics who were led by the Pope. The kirk used scripture to guide their Christian faith and preached in non-theological language so that ordinary people could understand God's message. Ireland at the time of Charles's accession was primarily Catholic, however there were pockets of Anglicans that had been granted lands and titles in order to oversee the native Irish. The majority of these Protestants by this time were situated in the north around Ulster. Indeed, these Protestants would play a role in keeping James II from regaining his crown in the Williamite war of 1689–91.

Due to his age, James, Duke of York, did not have much involvement during the Civil Wars between his father and his three kingdoms of Scotland, Ireland and England until the spring of 1642. Before that point he had been residing in his small household based at Richmond Palace in the county of Surrey. During the summer of 1642, the young Duke of York joined the king, in the second city of England, York.

In July of 1642, Charles received intelligence that the governor of the city of Hull, Sir John Hotham, would be willing to turn the city over to the king's cause if he arrived with a suitably strong retinue of Royalist support. Earlier in the year, prior to the young duke's reunion with his father, Charles had attempted to take Hull, which was considered a strategically important city due to its logistical advantages of being close to the coast and having access to the North Sea. To have the city willing to surrender to royal hands voluntarily was too good an opportunity for the Royalist cause not to act upon. If went as the king hoped, it should have been a bloodless annexation with excellent strategic possibilities. Charles was able to gather 4,000 loyal and armed supporters comprising of 3,000 men on foot and the remaining 1,000 upon horseback. He also decided to bring the 8-year-old Duke of York with him.

On 3 July, the king and his men arrived at the outskirts of Hull and the venture did not go according to plan. Seemingly oblivious to the fact this might have been dangerous, Charles sent his young son in to the city of Hull with a group of his supporters, including the Elector Palatine, Charles Louis. This delegation was entering the city to greet the city governor, Sir John Horsham. Horsham in turn greeted the party and offered them refreshments. Once the delegation was well into the city and suspecting nothing, the city's defensive gates were locked and the young duke and his party were effectively taken as hostages. Naively, Charles had never considered that the easy 'surrender' would in fact be a potential trap. The delegation party were only to be held as hostages for two days, and were detained with the due respect and courtesy that deserved by royalty, while the two sides parleyed for their release. Horsham would pay the ultimate price as the Parliamentarians found both him and his son guilty of aiding the king and were seen as traitors.

Although Charles had 4,000 royal supporters with him, they were no military match for the well-armed and disciplined might of the Cromwellian New Model Army. The Royalists stood no chance against the impressive defensive walls of the city of Hull either. The king and his retinue could do nothing but wait nearby. A week after the start of siege, the Parliamentarians had managed to draft an additional 2,000 well-trained and armed men to Hull. During the stand off, thirty of the king's men were taken hostage. The siege eventually came to an end on 27 July when the Royalists lost their precious cannon and ammunition to the other side. Charles and his remaining men retreated to their northern base in York.

These events and his two days as a hostage remained with James, both during the years of his brother's reign and later during his brief reign as king. According to the historian John Callow, James felt that his father, the king, did not take action soon enough after he was taken hostage. This view did not alter – and it is highly unlikely that he would not have been told of the external circumstances later. It is important to remember that James was still a child when this happened and his perception of the situation from the point of view of a hostage did not realise that negotiating for the hostages' release kept both James and the Elector of Palatines safe, as well as preventing a potential massacre within the seventeenth-century streets of Hull. This belief that his father had taken too long to act is a great example of James's irrational, uncompromising and zealous impatience, which would contribute, along with his stubborn temperament, to his eventual downfall as king in late 1688.

Having not learnt his lesson at Hull, Charles I then brought both his sons and heirs to witness the Battle of Edgehill a few months later in October. This was an extremely risky move on the king's part because James was still only 9 years old and although Prince Charles was older, he was only a teenager and also the immediate heir to the Stuart throne. As the battle proceeded and started to go against the Royalists, and the Parliamentarians drew closer to the king and his sons, Charles eventually ordered the Prince of Wales and Duke of York be taken away to safety.

It was considered that the two princes would be most secure in the Royalist stronghold of the university city of Oxford. This was where the king and his supporters had made their base camp and headquarters. Even after the affair at Hull, and the risks he had taken at the Battle of Edgehill, Charles placed both heirs at risk again in the summer of 1643.

In the late spring and early summer of 1643, the Royalists enjoyed a run of luck in their campaign. They even had some defectors from the Parliamentarian side, most notably Nathaniel Fiennes who surrendered to Prince Rupert of the Rhine. So when the intelligence came to the royal camp that the governor of Gloucester, one Edward Massey Esquire, was highly likely to change alliance to the Royalists, the king wanted to follow it up again. And once again Charles naively failed to see the potential trap. The city of Gloucester was well placed strategically. The city would give the Royalists access to the coast via the River Severn and was close to the south of Wales. Charles and his supporters were eager to take the chance and he took both his eldest sons to witness what he had hoped would be his biggest a triumph to date.

Upon arriving from Oxford, the two sides started official negotiations with Mr Massey the city governor; for some unknown reason, on 10 August, Edward Massey and the city of Gloucester rejected all the terms offered by the Royalists. Skirmishes started outside the walls of the city and once again Charles and his supporters found themselves in a siege situation.

Both the Prince of Wales and the Duke of York were taken to a nearby manor, Matson House as the Royalist forces started to work out how to take the city – this time by force. The siege was eventually ended by the weather; summer storms ruined the attack plans so the king and his party reluctantly retreated back to their southern base of Oxford. The young James was unimpressed by his father's lack of action. Even though still a boy, James was clearly more military minded than his overly cautious father.

Between 27 May and 4 June 1644 the Parliamentarians made a further attempt to take Oxford, which also failed; they made another failed attempt almost exactly a year later in 1645. In April 1646 they made a third attempt and began by trying to control which goods entered the city, forcing the city to use whatever provisions they had in their reserves. Having being targeted before, the city had been preparing for such an event. The New Model Army, under the leadership of General Sir Thomas Fairfax, also began discreetly transporting fifty kegs of gunpowder close to the city.

In mid-April there was a skirmish with cannon fire near the manor house of Woodstock, located close to Oxford, and a hundred Parliamentarians were killed, but this did not put them off. The manor was able to hold out against the soldiers for ten days before surrendering on 26 April. Following the loss of Woodstock, Charles decided to remove himself from Oxford; the king's departure did not ease the Parliamentarians grip on Oxford – if anything it made conditions for the citizens much worse. Freedom of movement in and out of the city by the scholars and tradesmen had by this point stopped and the city went into a lockdown siege on 1 May 1646.

Eleven days into the siege, Fairfax sent a request to the governor of Oxford, Sir Thomas Glemham; he wanted to bring the situation to an end and for Oxford to surrender. Glemham sent Fairfax a response three days later after consulting with the Privy Council asking that both parties meet to parley on 18 May. In the four days prior to their talks, the Royalists in the city destroyed all their documentation to avoid it falling into Parliamentarian hands. The discussions started on schedule on 18 May 1646, and the two sides debated and negotiated well into June. The king wanted to be sure that the people of Oxford, who had been so loyal to him, were not unduly or cruelly punished. After a month of negotiations an agreement was signed on 20 June within Christ Church College, and Parliament received the keys to the city from Glemham five days later.

One of the much negotiated terms of the Siege of Oxford was over what to do with James. It was finally agreed that he should be placed into the custody of the Parliamentarians. All of his household and servants were changed to parliament approved staff. The Parliamentarian hoped they would be able to influence the young prince so that parliament played a key role in the business of the state. Oh the irony. James's new guardian was Algernon Percy, Earl of Northumberland. The Duke of York joined his younger sisters, Princess Elizabeth and Princess Mary, who were also under the care and guardianship of the Earl of Northumberland and housed within the royal palace of St James, in London.

As well as this big change in James's life, he and his brother Charles would see their older German cousins, Princes Rupert of the Rhine, Maurice and Charles Louis, the Elector Palatine, exiled from English shores. The three nephews of Charles I had been leading Royalists for the king's cause and played key roles in several battles. The Parliamentarians told the three international royals an on 26 June they had ten days to leave the UK. The loss of these young European princes would be another blow for the king. For James his older cousins were both princely and military role models.

If the Parliamentarians thought the Duke of York would be an easy prisoner like his younger sisters then they greatly underestimated his personality and temperament; he already had his own fixed and stubborn opinions on the matters of monarchy, the divine right of kings, the role of royalty and military matters. If anything, James's time under the guardianship of the Earl of Northumberland can only have served to achieve the opposite to what the Parliamentarians had hoped, and cemented the young Duke of York's views further.

Although the Parliamentarians had an agenda for James, the royal siblings lived at St James's Palace in comfort and to the standard that would have been expected for royal children. Parliament gave Northumberland money to go towards their care and the earl even topped this up from his own personal wealth. (This may have been remembered later when the monarchy was restored, as Northumberland was one of the few Parliamentarians able to change allegiance and suffer no punishment for his political stance during the Civil Wars and interregnum under Cromwell.)

During the Duke of York's time at St James's Palace he learned that his father, the king, had been captured and was being held at Carisbrooke Castle near Newport. Charles I had been captured on 13 November 1647, just one month after the Duke of York had turned 14 years old. Upon hearing this, the teenage James is said to have grabbed a nearby bow and arrow and aimed it at the servant bearing news. Fortunately, other servants were able to overpower him and grab the bow before he was able to fire it. This is an early example of James's rash actions caused by his quick temper; a trait that was evident later throughout his brother Charles's reign as king, and also during his own brief reign. It was a side to his personality that would eventually contribute towards his fall from grace and the loss of his crowns.

During 1647, the Parliamentarians moved their hostage King Charles from Newport to the royal residency of Hampton Court Palace, Surrey, via the Berkshire town of Maidenhead. Northumberland was particularly keen upon this move as it would allow the royal children to visit their father and surprisingly, the parliament did grant permission for the king to see his children.

During these private meetings, the king encouraged his son to find a way to escape St James's palace and to get to mainland Europe for safety. The Duke of York would have had a couple of safe options in Europe; one was France as his mother, Queen Henrietta Maria, was of course French, and the other was the Netherlands, where his sister Princess Mary now lived with her husband William II of Orange, the stadtholder of the Dutch Republic. (His sister and her husband were the parents of William III of Orange, who would later go on to marry James's own daughter, also a Mary. William III would eventually depose James II during the Glorious Revolution of late 1688).

The Duke of York did successfully escape his virtual prison at St James's Palace in spring 1648. This escape could not have happened without help, which came from Joseph Bampfield a Royalist spy within St James's Palace. The daring escape took place on the evening of 20 April 1648. While playing hide and seek with his younger royal sibling, James was able to sneak out of the palace and made his way to St James's Park, where he met up with other associates of Bampfield. There he changed into women's clothes to look like a girl and travelled with these men up the Thames to meet up with a Dutch ship to take him to safety. The Duke of York arrived on 23 April 1648 in Flushing, also known as Vissingen, a naval port off the Netherlands in the province of Zeeland. James Duke of York, was safe once again.

During the first few months on the European mainland, James stayed within the safety of the Abbey of St Armand, home to a community of Benedictines located in the north of France. This place of safety was at the suggestion of his Catholic mother, Queen Henrietta Maria. It is highly likely that this is when the Duke of York embarked on his personal road to Damascus and explored the Catholic faith. This would eventually become very problematic and cost him a great deal.

In the summer of 1648, fighting between the Royalists and the Parliamentarians restarted and the Royalists were crushed by the might of the Parliamentarians' New Model Army. Hope was starting to dwindle for King Charles, his well-meaning and loyal supporters were no military match for the disciplined and well equipped New Model Army. Charles realised the only course of action left to him was to resume negotiations with his enemy. Although Parliament was willing to restart talks with the king, Cromwell wasn't; he was fed up of trying to negotiate with a man he saw as an autocratic oppressor. So, in early December 1648, Cromwell spearheaded what was effectively a military coup within parliament. This became known as the 'Pride's Purge' after Colonel Thomas Pride, the man in charge of the removal and arrest of MPs who were in favour of negotiations. The remaining MPs who were in agreement with Cromwell and the New Model Army, became known as the Rump Parliament.

Charles, who was being held on the Isle of Wight, was moved back to mainland England and on to Windsor Castle. In January 1649, he was formally charged with Treason against England and her people (note just England, not Scotland or Ireland) as he had used his role as king to pursue a course of action – the unification of the Anglican church – for personal reasons rather than for the good of the nation and in doing so, he had caused civil divisions that resulted in harmful civil war. The penalty for his treason was death.

Regardless of what the outcome had been, this would have been a landmark moment in the history of England, Great Britain and for sovereigns around the world. Very few people would have had the boldness or courage to execute an anointed king, thus making Oliver Cromwell one of history's most audacious figures. This was not the first time a monarch had been tried for treason. Charles's grandmother, the infamous Mary Queen of Scots, who had been forced to abdicate from the Scottish throne was also tried for treason for her involvement in the Babington Plot in 1586. Likewise, Lady Jane Grey, had her brief nine-day reign declared void and unlawful because she was never crowned, thus she was tried as a citizen rather than as a monarch.

King Charles I's trial was held at Westminster Hall, and started on 20 January 1649. This piece of judicial theatre was overseen by the solicitor general, John Cook. During his show trial Charles maintained that, as he was the monarch, and because he had been chosen by God, he was of a higher authority than the court that was trying him. His argument was that no man could try a monarch appointed by God. This was the same argument used by his grandmother, Mary Queen of Scots, during her trial in 1586. As a result, Charles refused to declare a plea of guilty or not guilty. Instead of halting the proceedings the court decided to continue as if he had pleaded guilty. In all, the trial took seven days and on 27 January 1649, the court found the king, Charles I of England, guilty of treason against England and the court proceeded to pass the sentence of death. In total fifty-nine men found the king guilty and would sign his death warrant.

Charles did not have to wait long to face the executioner's axe. On 30 January, on a specially erected raised platform draped in black cloth, located outside Banqueting House in Whitehall, Charles I would make history, losing his head and the Crown of England.

Given the events witnessed by James, Duke of York, during the last few years of his father's life, there is little wonder, in my opinion, that James would go on to develop such ridged and strongly held beliefs on surrounding sovereignty, kingship and the Divine Rights of Kings. Sadly, unlike his brother Charles II, James did not learn from his father's errors; he too lacked the judgement, patience and the understanding of when it was important to compromise.

The First Exile and Military Career until 1658

After Charles I lost the Civil Wars and subsequently his head in 1649, the new king, Charles II, and James, the Duke of York, were safely on continental Europe. The royal siblings were to spend much of the next decade without a permanent home or position. For the adolescent James, this time would have been vital in shaping who he would become as a man, through the experience and people he encountered.

James had escaped St James's palace and the wardenship of the 10th Earl of Northumberland on 20 April 1648 and was now in the safety of his sister's court at The Hague. Charles had escaped England before his brother and the prince was safely with his mother at the French court. Up to this point, James's life had been a turbulent one, but during the early days of this exile, he was surrounded by strong male role models. One of the people the now 15-year-old duke became particularly attached to was Colonel Joseph Bampfield, who had also orchestrated the duke's daring escape from London to the Netherlands.

James was the given the honorary title of the Lord High Admiral of the British Royal Navy, and being James as well as being 15 years old, he took every opportunity to exercise his authority and remind people of his title. The role of Lord High Admiral of Charles's navy was meant to be the responsibility of Bampfield, but he was ineffective and lazy so Charles gave the responsibility to their cousin, Prince Rupert of the Rhine. When Bampfield lost his standing and the advantages of his position, as well as the support of Charles, he decided to turn spy for the Parliamentarians and made contact with their spymaster, John Thurloe.

James was unhappy with his brother's decision to put Rupert in to the acting role of Lord Admiral and saw this as a personal slight against him. It was this spoilt and childish attitude that caused Charles to order that the Duke of York remain upon shore in September 1648 when royal vessels took part in sea trials. The parental like authority assumed by Charles over his younger brother caused tensions between the two siblings at the very time when they should have been uniting together. Although James was still just a teenager and can perhaps be forgiven for his immaturity, he was resentful of Charles's guidance and authority, taking it as a personal attack. Unfortunately, as he grew into an adult he failed to grow out of this immaturity and remained over sensitive and prone to outbursts.

At the beginning of 1649, the Duke of York left the refuge of his sister's court at The Hague to join his mother and brother in Paris. It was not long after he had arrived in the heart of his family at the French court that James heard of the fate of his father the late King Charles I. Sadly there are no accounts as to how the young duke reacted to such traumatic and deeply personal news.

Exile during this period was not all doom and gloom for James. He travelled back and forth from Paris and The Hague. In later months of 1649, he accompanied Charles to the Channel Islands were the brothers were able to have time to be young men. Among the activities they enjoyed together were sailing, fishing and shooting. Given their age and who they were, they no doubt enjoyed womanising as well. This boys bonding trip came to an end when Charles left for Scotland in an attempt to be crowned and get back his other thrones. There are similarities between Charles going to Scotland in 1650 and when James himself would go to Ireland in 1689 on the same mission to try and regain his thrones.

In a bid to give his younger brother a little more responsibility, Charles left him to take over the small garrison of men who were stationed on the Channel Islands. Not surprisingly, this responsibility proved too much of a challenge for the inexperienced teenage duke and he quickly wrote and requested to be relieved not long after

Charles had left. After returning to his own household, James was frustrated with his lot. Even in normal circumstances teenagers get frustrated and sometimes struggle to find direction, so it's no wonder that a teenage Duke of York, with everything he had witnessed and been through, and without a steady parent or guardian, struggled with appropriate responses – particularly at challenging and difficult times.

Possibly influenced by his royal cousin Prince Rupert, or from all the things he had witnessed as a child during the Civil Wars, James decided to follow a military career. The options to a prince, particularly a prince down on his luck like James, were limited. His best options would have been entering the clergy or the military. Ironically, it may have made more sense for James to have entered the clergy, especially when we see how he felt in the later years of his life. The duke's first taste of being a military man was in the early 1650s when he went to seek the Duc de Lorraine. Initially James and the Duc de Lorraine worked well together, however within a year James had out-stayed his welcome and usefulness to the Duc and was forced to return to his sister's court at The Hague. On this visit James met his sister Mary's new son, William; this baby would one day would be his son-in-law and depose him from his thrones in England, Scotland and Ireland.

Upon James's return to Paris Charles and Henrietta Maria put Sir Edward Hyde in charge of ameliorating the Duke of York. Hyde was the best they had in the absence of any other father figure to undertake this task. It is somewhat ironic, as Hyde would later become James's father-in-law when he married his daughter, Anne around the time of the Restoration.

The Duke of York was probably always going to struggle to find his place in court, society, life – in his position as the royal spare. This was made harder as the younger brother of a king without his thrones or crown and with no income. This made James a less attractive marriage match. He needed to find his place in the world and, having briefly tasted what life as a soldier was like, James Duke of York was admitted into the French army to seek adventure and his fortune!

From late April 1652 James found a place with one of the seventeenth century's highly acclaimed and most successful French generals, Henri de la Tour d'Auvergne, Viscount of Turenne. Over a four year period, James demonstrated that he was an instinctive soldier, brave to the point of reckless of his personal safety, observant and gallant. The Duke of York was active during battles as part of a cavalry unit in his role as junior staff officer. This hard work was rewarded with promotions and the duke would become indispensable to the aging Turenne, acting as a sharper and younger set of eyes during important exercises and battles. This arrangement was equally beneficial to James, as he was learning first hand from one of the best military men in France, and of the time. Having had very few stable male role models, James must have felt security and support from such a figure for the first time in his life.

By 1654 York had proved himself enough to have been awarded the promotion to the rank of Lieutenant General. During his four campaigns with the French army, under the mentorship, routine and discipline of Turenne he had matured from a lost, immature youth into a responsible prince, duke and man with a sense of self-worth, direction and purpose. Even that most fastidious of critics Sir Edward Hyde is said to have commented upon the change in James and how the French army had made the duke into a man stating he had, 'Much grown and improved', high praise indeed from Hyde (*The Making of King James II – The Formative Years of a Fallen King* Callow, J. p.87)

This new happiness would to change in the autumn of 1655, when French politics would make things difficult for James. The French diplomat and chief minister to Louis XIV, Giulio Raimondo Mazzarino – better known as Cardinal Jules Mazarin – sort to parley with Cromwell's interregnum government; as a consequence, James and his mother, the dowager queen Henrietta Maria, were in a politically and socially difficult position. Charles urged his brother to leave his beloved French army and take a position with the Spanish army based in Flanders instead.

For personal rather than political reasons, James was reluctant to leave the comrades and men he had served with over the last four campaign seasons. The French army was a sort of family to him and he had also just earned his promotion to Lieutenant General. There was no guarantee he would be accepted at that position in a new army – one that had formerly been his enemy. It is also worth noting James was still only in his very early twenties.

There were other reasons for this request from Charles, not just because Mazarin was working with Cromwell. Charles had relocated his court to Brussels, at the heart of Spanish Flanders, and had been negotiating and working on recruiting Spain to help him regain his lost kingdoms from Cromwell. Charles needed his younger brother to defect to the Spanish to help with his plans to woo the Spanish – Mazarin's actions were just a good excuse to request this.

In true James fashion, he was not going to give in easily. Initially he argued that he should not be made to leave his position within the French army as he had not personally been named within the agreements made between Charles and the Spanish. He felt so strongly about this issue that in January 1657, after having spent the festive period at his brother's court in Flanders, James took the drastic and somewhat rash action of attempting to return to France and Turenne. He left the Flanders' court of his brother with a small group of comrades to attempt this defiance. When Charles learnt of his brother's scheme, he attempted to lure him back and to abandon his plans to rejoin Turenne with a secure offer from the Spanish army; headstrong and stubborn, James rejected this attempt at reconciliation from his brother. Charles did not have to wait long before his younger brother returned, however. By the following month, February 1657, James decided to reconcile with Charles. Given the royal brothers' situation, the most likely cause of this swift change of heart was his lack of finances rather than his good will. He agreed to return to Charles's court in Bruges, providing he was able to have full control over his personal household.

Although Charles and James did not always agree with each other over matters regarding state, politics or personal choices, the one thing they did unite over was finding a way to get Charles back on his thrones. The one thing about James that you cannot fault is that he was a fiercely loyal person and although accepting the position within the Spanish army affected him personally, he would have eventually seen how this could aid his brother in this goal.

It would not be a smooth transition for James, as he reluctantly defected to his former enemy on the battlefield. James had brought with him men who had been loyal and served under him in the French army, and as expected they soon started bickering with their new Spanish comrades. James also was unhappy; he did not like the Spanish staff officers and the way in which they worked, compared to their French counterparts. He spent two fighting campaign seasons within the Spanish army and during that time he fought in the Spanish defeat at the Battle of Dunes, 1658. The badly organised and divided Spaniards lost to James's former friend and mentor Turenne and the French's new ally, the English Republicans. This particular defeat must have stung James, firstly being beaten by his old friends, but to rub salt into that wound, they were working with the very side that had executed his father – and were keeping his brother from his rightful throne. James returned to his brother's court after the defeat at Dunes, and it was then that he learnt of Cromwell's death, in September 1658.

James's military career during that first exile period of his life was a defining moment for him as he changed from a teenager into a man. During this time he experienced support, discipline and routine, as well as victories with the French. During his battle of wills with Charles, he exercised and expressed his need for independence and he would also learn the hard lessons of having to do the right thing and work with people he disliked, as well as experiencing defeat in both a military and personal context. It also seems that this short period in James's life might have been one of the few times he was personally content as a man and had found a role for himself. He experienced a sense of great pride from his personal successes; he was accepted as a man, rather than a prince, spare heir or a duke.

The Politics of the Restoration
1660–1685

To understand the politics that affected and shaped the future James II & VII, it is important to have a comprehension of the political history of the early Restoration and the differences between the political factions and key players. The problem after the republican years under Cromwell was that the returning monarch, and the ideas of monarchy, had not evolved whereas the institution of government and the role of parliament had. If changes had been made in 1660 at the Restoration, James *might* have been able to hold on the throne and remained king regardless of his religious preference. The social and political backdrop of the reign of Charles II would be the one James inherited in 1685 and so it is an important to this book.

The one thing that both English republicanism and the Restoration Stuart monarchy had in common was that both establishments did not separate state from religion which what had been at the crux of political discord for British monarch since the Reformation, regardless of whether they were Catholic or Protestant.

There was a brief honeymoon period after Charles regained the Crown, and after years of harsh Puritan dictatorship under Cromwell's republic; the majority of Britain was relieved to have a 'merry' monarch. After the initial idyll, Britain found herself in an uneasy political balance of trust and cooperation between king and parliament, primarily over the issues of money, religion and later on in his reign, the succession. Charles and his parliament tolerated each other until the start of what became known as the Exclusion Crisis, a political storm centred around trying to exclude the Duke of York from inheriting his brother's throne because of his Catholic faith. It was during this crisis that the political balance shifted and it reached a point where it looked like the Earl of Shaftesbury and Duke of Buckingham could potentially get their way. This made Charles feel like he had no other choice but to exercise his right to dismiss parliament. He did this in March 1681.

The Restoration's parliamentary sessions until late 1678 became known as the Cavalier Parliament. In 1679 and '80 there were no sessions called until the final session was called in Oxford in March 1681. Over the eighteen and half years of the Cavalier Parliament, there were eighteen parliamentary sessions held. In some ways, the Cavalier Parliament worked along similar lines to the one we are familiar with today. There were two houses, the Commons that were elected* and the Lords, made up of hereditary peers of the realm as well as Church of England bishops. The biggest difference between the Restoration's parliament and today's House of Commons is that there were no formalised or official political parties. Nor were there any leaders or ministers. Issues were debated by elected representatives and subsequently voted on based on an individual's views, morals, religious beliefs, or how it would affect their lives. The members of both the Houses of Commons and Lords roughly separated into two factions of ideas: the Court faction and the Country faction. Membership of these groups were transitory and dependent upon policy or the issue being debated at that time.

MPs who were part of the Country faction had a tendency to be pro-Protestant, both domestically and internationally, and protective of the rights of parliament and democracy; they would later become concerned about the monarch's encroachment of these political, social and parliamentary rights. Among the leading figures of this movement were Lord Cavendish, William Lord Russell and after 1674, Lord Shaftesbury and the Duke of Buckingham.

---

* The seventeenth-century definition of elected is not what we understand it to be today. The votes were limited to a very few of people; suffrage was not universal to all men, and women had no say at all.

The Court faction of MPs is harder to define. Firstly, they were not united in faith; having varied religious backgrounds, Catholics were more likely to be among these men. They had no united view on issues such as foreign policy. The one political concept that they all held firm and believed in was the powers and rights of the monarch. Many of the Court circle had fathers who had fought for the Cavaliers during the Civil Wars and some had been in exile with Charles during the frustrating period of Cromwell's interregnum. These men, like Charles, were generally pro-French in terms of foreign policy, as well as being more tolerant of other religious denominations such as Catholics and deserter denominations of Christianity such as the Quakers. The thought of excluding James from the throne due to his Catholic faith would have been irreconcilable to their politics, especially when the suggested alternative to the lawful heir was the king's illegitimate son the Duke of Monmouth, or 'Foreign' William of Orange. The Court faction was less open to a more 'democratic' form of government, believing in the idea of the divine right of kings and that a king should rule, and not rule alongside, or under, a politically dominant parliament. Compared to the Country faction, who were widely appealing to the populace at large, the Court faction were exactly as their name suggests; they were made up of a small, elitist minority close to the monarch. They were traditionalists and more worried about maintaining their favour with Charles than the good of the nation.

Then there were Privy Councillors who did not follow this political or moral pattern and this is why the Court faction is harder to define in ideology. For example, the Earl of Clarendon, Edward Hyde, was part of this group, but he was most certainly not tolerant of other religious denominations or pro-French. He was, however, a monarchist to the core of his political being. Included within Charles's Privy Council were: Thomas Clifford, 1st Baron Clifford of Chudleigh; Henry Bennet, 1st Earl of Arlington; George Villiers, 2nd Duke of Buckingham; Antony Ashley Cooper, 1st Baron Ashley and John Maitland, 1st Duke of Lauderdale. There were other men who were part of this circle, however, these five MPs were at the heart of this group. They were also a good mix of both the country and court fractions.

Edward Hyde, later the Earl of Clarendon, rose to be the primary adviser to Charles II until 1668. He would also become the maternal grandfather to two English queens: Mary II who reigned with her husband, William, and then Queen Anne. He started his political career as MP for Wootton Bassett in April 1640 and was an MP in the short parliament. Seven months later, when parliament reconvened in November of the same year, Hyde became MP for Saltash. Even though he would become one the most trusted advisers to both Charles I and II, Hyde started his political career as a temperate critic of Charles I.

From December 1641, Edward Hyde rose swiftly up the political ladder, and was appointed Chancellor of the Exchequer in February 1643. Among the royal circle, he had a reputation for being conservative in his politics. After the execution of the Charles I, Hyde joined Charles II in exile. He would become Charles's chief adviser and was rewarded for his dedication in 1658, when he was officially appointed Lord Chancellor. However, his conservative view which had kept Charles II afloat in exile would prove restrictive, boring and pompous in the opulent and frivolous court of the early years of the Restoration court. Hyde attracted powerful enemies within the Restoration court and its parliament. He fell from grace after a catalogue of problems – and rumours blaming him for them. This included the ridiculous accusation that he knew Queen Catherine was barren and that he was to blame for the Fire of London in 1666. His unpopularity was not helped by the political codes that bore his name. In the end the earl became a convenient scapegoat for the disastrous Anglo-Dutch wars. He was impeached in 1667 and forced into 'retirement' in Europe. He settled in the French city of Rouen, France, where he died, alone and gouty, in December 1674. His son would bring his mortal remains back to England so that they could be burial with status within Westminster Abbey. Edward Hyde, Earl of Clarendon did not, therefore, live to see his onetime son-in-law become king, or both his granddaughters triumphs at becoming the last two Stuart queens.

Hyde's political career clearly demonstrates how seventeenth-century politics was interwoven with ideas of religion. It helps the more secular twenty-first-century reader understand the political environment and thought process witnessed by the Duke of York, and might explain some of his decisions later as James II. The role that religious belief played in Restoration politics exasperated the divisions within parliament and the issues at hand – particularly the policy on succession. Politics with a religious undercurrent meant that Christian denominations turned against each other. England, Scotland and Wales were all Protestant nations and there was a genuine fear of Catholicism when it was practiced by those in politics and by those close to the monarchy. By converting to Rome during the Restoration, the then Duke of York was setting himself up for a difficult reign as James II & VII. (James Conversion to Catholicism is covered in more detail later in the book.)

This fear of Rome and the Catholic church was a legacy left over from the Reformation triggered by Henry VIII in the sixteenth century, as well as the wider European Reformation and subsequent counter-Reformation that ended up dividing Europe. The divisions within the European mainland created both allies and enemies for Britain. But the divisions within Europe also highlighted the link between Catholicism and Absolutism and tyranny. Charles and James's cousin, the French king Louis XIV, was a prime example of an absolute Catholic monarch. By comparison, Protestantism represented seventeenth-century ideas of a limited form of democracy and freedom of thought. Something that had been missing during the reign of Charles I and later during Cromwell's rule.

This Restoration political environment was largely created by Whig politician and prominent Exclusionist MP, Anthony Ashley Cooper, 1st Earl of Shaftesbury. Although he did not play a role in James II's reign, he was a key player within the Exclusion Crisis and the early Whig movement to such an extent that I would argue that his political spirit is evident and helped the make the Glorious Revolution possible in 1688.

Born in 1621, Cooper was orphaned by the age of 8, with a fortune and baronetcy. This sad beginning did not hinder him and he would go on to attend Exeter College, Oxford – though he left minus a degree, instead following a law career at Lincoln's Inn, London. This career opening was due to his first father-in-law, the 1st Baron Coventry. Cooper married Margaret Coventry in 1639 and through this marriage, he was able to enter politics at the age of 19 when he won his first parliamentary seat in the Short Parliament in spring 1640. He was the Member of Parliament for Tewkesbury & Gloucestershire.

The Short Parliament is rather an apt description for a parliament that lasted from 13 April until the 5 May 1640. It was the first parliament that Charles I had called in eleven years for the purpose of trying to impose Anglicanism upon Scotland and replacing the Scottish Kirk. Parliament refused to cooperate with the king and he duly dissolved the session when it became clear he would not get his way. Parliament had lasted just twenty-two days.

However parliament did not need to wait long before it was once again recalled by the Charles I. In November of the same year, just 6 months after dissolving the Short Parliament, Charles summoned his MPs again in what would become known as the Long Parliament. Although on the 3 November 1640, government resumed, the MPs had insured that the king could not again dissolve them without the agreement of the Houses of Commons. Consequently, this parliamentary session would officially go on and last throughout the Civil Wars, the interregnum under Oliver Cromwell and his son Richard right up until just before the restoration, when it was officially dissolved on 16 March 1660, ahead of Charles II returning to restore the monarchy to Britain.

In the autumn of the same year, Cooper was not asked to stand again for the same constituency as part of the Long Parliament elections. He tried to be re-elected to the Long Parliament through a by-election for Downton in Wiltshire, but despite winning the required number of votes he was blocked from entering the Commons by Denzil Holles who was aligned to Cromwell. Holles disliked Cooper's close links to the Royal household. Seventeenth-century ideas of democracy were vastly different to a modern understanding and winning the required number of votes did not guarantee that you were the MP – especially if you held unpopular views or connections. It was certainly a matter of who you knew and how you could influence them.

For the first two years of the Civil Wars, Cooper was loyal to the Royalists and Charles I. Eventually, his split from the Royalists was due to a disagreement with Prince Maurice of the Palatinate, the elder bother of Prince Rupert of the Rhine. The disagreement was because the prince had allowed his men to rampage through and sack the southern towns of Dorchester and Weymouth, after Cooper had given his word to the two towns that they would be spared from pillaging. Prince Maurice would go on to hold a grudge after an altercation between himself and Cooper. Subsequently, in a petty act of revenge, he attempted to block Cooper's promotion to Governor of Weymouth and Portland, claiming Cooper was too inexperienced. Ironically, Cooper appealed to his future rival, Edward Hyde, who helped him to take the position of Governor under the proviso that he resign after a dignified period of holding it, to appease the disgruntled prince and his 'concerns'.

By 1644, Cooper had changed allegiance and joined Cromwell. He resigned all his posts under Charles I, feeling that the king was under the influence of too many Catholics. It is easy to see why he would become a leading member of the Exclusionist cause during the Restoration. Cooper said that his conscience dictated that it was right to join the Parliamentarian cause to uphold the Protestant faith in England. In 1652, when he was appointed to the Hale Committee and the fact that Cooper, who was a political turncoat, had been asked to be part of a republican parliamentary committee, shows his skill at political survival. In 1653 Cromwell nominated him to stand in the election as the MPs for the county of Wiltshire. This parliamentary session was known as the Barebones Parliament or Little Parliament and during it, Cooper aligned himself with the moderate politicians, a good survival strategy.

Cooper was elected for Tewksbury in 1654, but his political alliance with Cromwell would soon deteriorate. By early 1655, Cooper was concerned that Cromwell was ruling through the fear and force of the New Model Army, rather than through his parliament. Cooper's decision to stand up to Cromwell would affect his political career until the Restoration. In 1656 he was excluded from forming part of the new government along with sixty-five other former MPs. This was because, along with the MPs, Cooper had signed a petition objecting to Cromwell's undemocratic behaviour – in their eyes, Cromwell was acting little better than Charles I had before the Civil Wars. This action would cost him two years of his political career before being forgiven by Cromwell and allowed to return to what would be Cromwell's last parliament in early 1658.

After Oliver Cromwell's death in late 1658, Cooper spoke against Richard Cromwell during the third Protectorate Parliament. When the New Model Army dissolved the Rump Parliament in autumn 1659, Cooper was an active member of a group who continued to meet regularly to discuss political ideas and how they saw the political future of Great Britain. These men eventually approached Sir George Monck who took the first steps towards restoring the monarchy, as this seemed to be the best solution to the political quagmire Britain was in. Cooper would be part of the company who went to The Hague to meet Charles and helped draw up the declaration of Breda. Ever the political survivor, Cooper would ensure that he received an official pardon for his political association with Cromwell's Commonwealth during the negotiations.

Within the new regime Charles had so much trust in Cooper as an ally and politician, that he took a prominent role in the trial and conviction of the regicides. In this role he used the Indemnity and Oblivion Act of 1660 to pardon some who may have committed crimes during the Civil Wars and interregnum. Not all were lucky and found themselves convicted of serious crimes committed during this time. These were mainly the men who would become known as regicides – and played an active role in bringing about the execution of Charles I. Some of the men whom Cooper helped to convict, had worked with alongside Cooper during the Cromwellian republic.

The issue of Cooper's dislike of the encroachment of Catholicism towards the British throne would resurface in Restoration politics as early as 1661 when he objected to Charles's choice of bride, Catherine of Braganza. However, his pro-Protestant politics would intensify when he met the illegitimate Duke of Monmouth for the first time in 1665, when they were introduced by none other than Charles II himself, during a visit to Cooper's estate in Wimborne, St Giles. The seeds of the Exclusion Crisis were sewn.

At the start of the 1670s Cooper fell out of favour with Charles; he was pushing the king to divorce Queen Catherine, as she was proving unable to conceive the much-needed male Stuart heir. Cooper raised this risky subject with Charles because of the Duke of York; James had recently converted to Catholicism and remarried a Catholic, Mary of Modena. As a result, Cooper feared that if the Duke of York inherited the throne and subsequently produced male issue, there would be a Catholic line of succession. A consequence of his putting pressure on Charles led to Cooper losing his position as Lord Chancellor. Although he had displeased the king over his opinions relating to Queen Catherine, Charles still rewarded him for his political support for the Royal Declaration of Indulgence. In the list of honours announced in April 1672, Anthony Ashley Cooper was honoured with the title Earl of Shaftesbury; which is how he is most commonly remembered.

The next important event that links Shaftesbury to the Duke of York's story happens in the following spring, when the Test Act became law. The act made it a legal requirement that all those in political or court offices must take the Protestant Anglican communion and renounce the act of transubstantiation, the central doctrine of the Catholic faith – the belief that the bread and wine used in Holy Communion turn into the literal body and blood of Jesus Christ. Shaftesbury was with the Duke of Monmouth when they were witnessed taking Anglican communion in the London church of St Clement Danes. Their witness was the imminent seventeenth-century 'scientist' John Locke, who was also Shaftesbury's personal doctor. The newly converted Catholic Duke of York refused to comply with the Test Act and lost his position as Lord High Admiral of the Royal Navy.

Politically, Shaftesbury had tried to ensure the Protestant line of succession and failed. The great political survivor would once more change political alliances and move away from the Court faction and towards the Country faction. This change became known during the new parliamentary session in January 1674, and the beginning of the Whig party can be traced to this point. Like minded politicians, who were opposed to a Catholic succession, including the Earl of Carlisle, the Earl of Salisbury, the Duke of Buckingham, Viscount of Halifax and Baron Holles, started to meet frequently away from parliament. They would meet and discuss the issues of succession at Holles's home. During these meetings, alternative policies are highly likely to have been discussed, including the exclusion of the Duke of York from the throne and the Duke of Monmouth, or William of Orange with York's eldest daughter, Mary as possible alternatives.

Shaftesbury went on to attack leading Catholics, focusing upon the Duke of York. One of the ideas that he tried to pass was to introduce a new law that would ensure that any of the Duke of York's subsequent legitimate children, from his second wife, Mary of Modena, should be raised in the Anglican communion, or face being excluded from inheriting the British throne. This did not come into being and the anti-Catholic faction were starting to become politically frustrated. They became so frustrated that they almost accused the Duke of York of high treason on the grounds that his religion was harmful to the throne and kingdom. Shaftesbury sadly did not live to see this become reality in law under the reign of William and Mary and the creation of the constitutional monarchy.

The king heard of these plots and decided to end the parliamentary session ensuring that the Duke of York was not accused of high treason. The consequences of his involvement cost Shaftesbury his place in the Privy Council, as well as the goodwill of the king. He was also exiled from London. Shaftesbury continued in this vein during the next parliamentary session of late 1675. During the chaos of the popish plot, Shaftsbury attempted to use this ant-Catholic wave to recruit more MPs to the exclusion cause.

After the Oxford Parliament (see below) was dissolved in March 1681, Shaftsbury was at a loose end. In July of the same year he was arrested and sent to the Tower of London on false accusations of high treason. He was acquitted of these charges but not long after his release thought it prudent to go into voluntary exile. He only lived in exile three months, dying in the Netherlands in January 1683.

The Earl of Shaftesbury is important to understanding James's failings as a king at the Glorious Revolution in 1688 because politically he was ahead of his time, seeing that parliament should take a strong role in running the country and that church and state should not be interwoven. Shaftesbury had lived through times of civil unrest, both socially and politically. This affected his strong political beliefs regarding the inheritance of the throne and the importance of maintaining the Anglican faith and the role of the monarch, and this can be traced throughout his political career.

* * *

Another leading Restoration political player was George Savile, Earl of Halifax. Halifax was something of a political free spirit. During his political career, he did not commit to one faction or idea in politics. He joined the Restoration court in 1660 and seems to have slipped in and out of Whitehall sporadically. However, he did have one passionate belief that was evident throughout his politics: his anti-Catholic stance. This meant that he had an intense dislike of the king's brother, the Duke of York. It is therefore quite surprising that during the Exclusion Crisis, Halifax helped Charles to defeat the Lords from passing the Exclusion Bill, especially in that he was the nephew of leading Exclusionist, Lord Shaftesbury. Halifax's allegiance would change in 1680. This was when he supported the idea that Monmouth should be the king's heir. There is no evidence that this was a long term association or that Halifax was anyway involved in the ill-fated Monmouth Rebellion of 1685. If he had been, James II would have taken this opportunity to be rid of one of his most ardent opponents. Halifax would go on to become one of the leading facilitators of the Glorious Revolution in 1688, which would finally see his nemesis James II deposed and William and Mary established as a new constitutional monarchy.

The first Exclusion Parliament lasted five months, from 6 March until 12 July 1679. Exclusion entered parliament because the Duke of York had been discovered to have been corresponding with both Rome and his cousin, King Louis XIV of France. The Commons felt these correspondences were potentially dangerous and could encourage conspiracies against the both the king and national Protestantism. Ironic as the king himself had entered into a secret treaty with Louis in 1670. Charles attempted to sooth his parliament by suggesting that any Catholic successors should have less freedoms as monarch than he had as a Protestant monarch. This did not pacify the hard-line Exclusionists, led by Shaftesbury. The first reading of the Exclusion Bill took place on 15 May 1679, with the second six days later on 21 May. When the House of Commons voted, the bill was passed comfortably by 207 votes to 127. To avoid the bill going any further, Charles dissolved parliament on 12 July.

The second Exclusion Parliament was called in October 1679. The reason why Charles recalled parliament was because he had failed to secure further funds from the French and he needed more money. But Parliament knew that they had power over the king and was not going to let this opportunity pass. Charles would prorogue his rebellious parliament six more times during 1680 on: 26 January, 17 May, 1 July, 23 August, and finally, 21 October 1680. Despite Charles's efforts, the Exclusionists had great support for their cause in both the upper and lower chambers of parliament. The Exclusion Bill passed three readings in the Commons and made it to the Lords. With help from the Earl of Halifax, the king got his way when the Lords voted against Exclusion. The bill failed sixty-three to thirty.

The final Exclusion Parliament and last parliament of Charles's reign, was called by the king in March 1681 and is known as the Oxford Parliament. There is a detailed explanation of this important parliamentary session in the chapter entitled 'The End of the Restoration Reign'. This would be the last time a British monarch would wield such powers within a parliamentary setting.

Charles was able to dissolve this last parliament because he had finalised the Secret Treaty of Dover, the terms of the treaty granted Charles a down payment of £40,000 and then an annual pension of £115,000 for the next three years, on the proviso that he did not recall parliament. It is worth noting that the Duke of York may have thought that this would be an arrangement he would continue with his cousin, Louis of XIV of France, upon the death of his brother Charles. In a last ditch attempt to pacify the Exclusion faction of his government, Charles suggested that when he died and James inherited the throne, William and Mary should rule as regents and that James be king in name alone, with none of powers of the monarchy that he himself exercised. This did not go down well with his brother, and the suggestion was unsurprisingly rejected by parliament. In just a week, the last parliament of Charles II's reign was dissolved.

* * *

Thomas Osborne, who would become Lord Danby as well as take the title 1st Duke of Leeds, belonged to the Court faction. Like may from the gentry class, Osborne's family had been Royalists during the Civil Wars. In 1661 he became the High Sheriff of York and was elected as MP for York in the 1665 elections. His connection at court was George Villiers, Duke of Buckingham, and the two joined forces against the conservative and stuffy Edward Hyde, Earl of Clarendon. In 1668, Osborne was appointed Treasurer to the Royal Navy and would rise within the admiralty. In 1673, he was created Viscount Osborne and become a Privy Councillor. The following year Charles made him the Earl of Danby and he would be known as Lord Danby at court. He was admitted into the Order of the Garter in 1677.

Danby was Anglican and disliked both Catholics and other Christian denominations such as the Quakers. Although he was initially against Clarendon, he did support the Test Act, and believed those closest to the king should be of the Anglican communion. He felt so strongly about this that he spearheaded a political campaign that become known as the Compton Census in 1676. The Compton Census's purpose was to determine the number of non-Church of England Christians within each diocese in England. When the results were studied it showed that to every twenty-three Anglicans there was one non-Anglican Christian. Furthermore, when broken down specifically into Anglicans to Catholics, there were 179 Anglicans to one Catholic.

Danby was so convinced that the nation – and specifically the Catholics – were plotting against Charles, that he attempted to close the emerging and thriving coffee house culture in 1676. Danby claimed that these establishments were where dissenters and Catholics met to plot treason. This crusade did not last long or get very far, however. From 1674 Danby had regular correspondence with William of Orange and would help broker the marriage agreement between William and Mary, the Duke of York's daughter. From the evidence seen already it is easy to see how Danby would become one of the major players in the Glorious Revolution of 1688. However, before he triumphantly deposed James in favour of William and Mary, Danby fell out of favour with Charles II and subsequently found himself impeached.

Ralph Montagu was one of Charles's secretaries of state and would be sacked by the king for upsetting his current favourite mistress, Barbara Villiers. In revenge he started plotting against the anti-French and anti-Catholic Lord Danby. Montagu managed to get himself elected to the House of Commons where he set about attacking Danby. On 20 December 1678 the speaker of the house read two very damning letters written by Danby that consequently got him impeached. This was very serious as in the seventeenth century, impeachment could cost you your life. Although the House of Commons had voted that Danby was guilty, the House of Lords were less inclined to do so. They had not reached their decision when parliament was terminated on 30 December 1678. For now Danby was still free and safe. In March 1679, he relinquished his treasury role. Charles must have realised that Montagu had been causing trouble and he compensated Danby by awarding him the title of Marquess and granted him a royal pardon – drawing a line under his impeachment for the time being.

Parliament were still not happy and the Commons issued a bill of attainder against Danby despite his royal pardon. A bill of attainder is an act of parliament that finds an individual guilty of a crime without a trial, usually reserved for obvious cases of high treason such as rebellion. On the 21 April, he was arrested and brought to the Tower of London. Danby's arrest and the legality of the royal pardon in cases of impeachment would later be ratified by law in 1701 in the Act of Settlement. As a result, Danby found himself residing at the Tower of London for the next five years. While in the Tower, Danby attempted to get justice by writing and appealing to parliament, the king and through the courts. Eventually it would be Judge Jeffreys (who became infamous due to the Bloody Assize in 1685) that eventually granted him his freedom at the high bail cost of £40,000, in February 1684.

After the death of Charles and the accession of James, Danby returned to the House of Lords. Considering Danby's well known anti-Catholic stance he was initially supportive of his new Catholic king. This did not last long, and as James's reign continued, he found himself more and more disillusioned. In the summer of 1687, Danby was back in contact with William of Orange and a year later he was one of seven leading men of the realm who signed the official document, inviting William of Orange and Mary to take the throne. Thomas Osborne, Earl of Danby, was important to the politics that both shaped the later part of the Restoration reign, and was proactively involved in the Glorious Revolution that would topple James II in 1688.

* * *

George Villiers, 2nd Duke of Buckingham, was one of the seventeenth century's most unlikely political reformers. He spent most of his childhood growing up alongside the royal princes Charles and James. He was a few years older than them and consequently more active during the Civil Wars on the side of the Royalists. When he lost his brother Francis, Buckingham managed to escape to the Protestant territory of the Netherlands.

During his time in exile with Charles, he would be granted the honour of the Knight of the Garter and stood on the exiled king's Privy Council. Buckingham had hoped that the Scottish Presbyterians would help Charles defeat the Cromwellian Republicans. However their endeavours to woo the Scots were unsuccessful. Before escaping back to mainland Europe, Charles and his supporters went south to England but were defeated at the hands of the New Model Army during the Battle of Worcester in 1651.

During the first part of the 1650s, Buckingham lost favour with Charles after opening negotiations with the Republican government under Cromwell. He was also indiscreet with Charles's widowed sister Mary, who was the mother of William of Orange. Exile became too much for Buckingham so when he was given the opportunity to return to England in 1657 he took it. It was a risk, he was known to have been part of Charles's exiled court. The reason for his return was to marry. On 15 September 1657, he married Lady Mary, the daughter of Lord Fairfax. Cromwell was suspicious of Buckingham and had him placed under house arrest in April 1658. Four months later, Buckingham slipped past his guards and escaped. He was soon recaptured and this time he was placed in the Tower of London until 1659, when Lord Fairfax put up a bail of a staggering £20,000.

At the Restoration, Lord Fairfax changed his political allegiance and he and Buckingham were once again part of the royal circle. Buckingham was given the privileged position of the Gentleman of the Bedchamber, making him one Charles's top courtiers and soon one of the wealthiest men in England. Not everyone was pleased to see Buckingham's return to favour; the Earl of Clarendon, the Chancellor, was not amused and was able to persuade the king to limit Buckingham's influence. In the process, Clarendon made himself an enemy that would bring about his own fall from power and favour.

Buckingham's behaviour within the House of Lords found him returning to the Tower from 27 June 1667 for twenty days. Once again Charles did not learn and Buckingham soon regained favour, becoming part of a political group known as the Cabal. This group included: 1st Baron Clifford of Chudleigh, Thomas Clifford; 1st Earl of Arlington, Henry Bennet; Earl of Shaftesbury, Antony Ashley Cooper; Duke of Lauderdale, John Maitland and 2nd Duke of Buckingham, George Villiers. The name Cabal came from their Initials Clifford, Arlington, Buckingham, Ashley and Lauderdale. Politics within the Cabal of Privy Councillors was not just national and international, its agenda was often personal and petty in nature too. At the root of most of these political problems, both large and small, was the issue of Christian denomination. Despite their differences the Cabal, with help and encouragement from Buckingham, was eventually able to impeach, Clarendon.

The House of Commons started debating the alleged crimes of Edward Hyde, Earl of Clarendon, on 26 October 1667. His career and speeches were examined and reinterpreted to fit Buckingham's agenda. Accusations of high treason were also thrown around, however the House of Commons found nothing to solidify such a serious and capital crime against Clarendon. On 18 December 1667 Buckingham won, Clarendon was impeached on seventeen so-called misdemeanours – but the biggest theme of his so-called 'crimes' seems to have been advising caution.

During the 1670s, Buckingham stirred up opposition to the queen, Catherine of Braganza, because she had failed to give Charles a male heir. It is at this point that Buckingham's exclusionist views towards James, then Duke of York, were clear for all to see.

In 1678–80, Buckingham manipulated the chaos and fear caused by Titus Oates's false Popish Plot. Its anti-Catholic agenda suited Buckingham but he was not active within the Exclusionists and was unscathed by their attempts to bar the Duke of York from the throne, both legal and illegal. He did survive Charles II by two years but choose to stay away from court in his Yorkshire home. He died 16 April 1687. Buckingham is important due to his anti-Catholic politics in the Restoration. His actions encouraged the atmosphere of anti-Catholic fear that would eventually spark the Glorious Revolution to remove James II. Although he, like Shaftsbury, did not live to see the fruits of their labour, their political spirit can be seen in what took place in late 1688.

As the different political fractions started to become clearer with stronger political aims the Court and Country factions developed into seedling political parties – the Country Faction the Whigs, and the Court Faction the Tories. As the political landscape was evolving, James inherited his throne and tried to halt this evolution by traditional methods which appeared out of date and autocratic. The seeds of the Glorious Revolution germinated during Charles II's reign and the key players of the time, Clarendon, Halifax, Shaftesbury, Danby and Buckingham, all played their part – even if some of them were no longer alive to see this great change, politically and socially. It did not help that James was less politically minded and emotionally more volatile than his brother Charles had been. He was also impulsive, impatient and had a stubborn streak. When he lost his throne to his nephew, William of Orange and his daughter Mary II, Britain embarked upon a new way to rule – through a constitutional monarchy. Sadly, the French monarchy did not learn from our monarchy and 144 years after the execution of Charles I, they too executed a monarch and his wife.

Marriage to Anne Hyde and the Birth of Two Queens

One thing the royal house of Stuarts did not lack was libido. Whether it was Mary Queen of Scots, James I of England, or Charles II – who was the most notorious of them all – these royals had a healthy sexual appetite. James, Duke of York, was no exception. During his lifetime he married twice, the first of his wives being Anne Hyde. She was the daughter of Edward Hyde, later Earl of Clarendon, adviser first to James's father and then his brother's most trusted adviser and chancellor. Anne Hyde would give James eight children during their short marriage, though only two of these children reached adulthood; both were female and both went on to hold the title of Queen of England.

Anne Hyde was born on 12 March 1637, in the Berkshire town of Windsor. Four years following her birth, her father, who was then a lawyer, had managed to establish himself as an informal advisor to Charles I. This was rather an impressive career move as Hyde had previously expressed anti-monarchy opinions when he was a member of parliament. Little is known of Anne's very early childhood. It was during this time that the early part of the Civil Wars that took place in Scotland, Ireland and England. However, we can safely assume that she was with her mother, Frances Aylesbury, and her other siblings while her father worked within the court helping and advising the ill-fated Charles I.

After the defeat of Charles I and his execution, the Hyde family decided it was safest to relocate into voluntarily exile in Europe. The family had more options than most due to the support that Edward Hyde had shown the late king during the civil conflicts. So in early summer 1649, four months after the king's execution upon Whitehall, the Hyde family arrived in the Netherlands. By this time Edward Hyde had been made Chancellor and had continued supporting the new exiled monarch, Charles II. The new king's sister, Princess Mary Stuart of Orange, would help the family settle into their new life. Princess Mary had been grateful to Edward Hyde for his support of her late father and his continued support of her brother Charles II. She offered the family a home, rent free, in the port town of Breda. This would not be the only help that Mary would extend to the family or to Anne Hyde.

In 1654 Mary, the Princess of Orange, would take Anne on as a member of her household as a vacancy had opened up due to one of her waiting ladies dying of smallpox. Her father, the conservative Edward, was not particularly pleased his eldest daughter would be leaving his wife, Frances, with all her younger siblings. Leaving the family home would not have been Edward Hyde's only anxiety as his daughter would be entering into the close circles of the Orange court, which had links with the libertine court of the exiled Charles II. Charles had already fathered his first illegitimate child, James, Duke of Monmouth, by 1654. It is easy to see why Hyde would have been uncomfortable with the thought of his daughter mixing in close proximity to these circles. This contact with Charles II's amorous exiled court would have increased the following year as Princess Mary had become a widow, with her a young son. The baby was already the new William III of Orange.

One of the first opportunities that Anne might have had to meet her future husband may well have been when Princess Mary and her household visited her mother, the formidable Henrietta Maria of France, dowager queen of England and widow of Charles I, at the French royal court. This visit of several months in 1655, would have given Anne Hyde plenty of time to mingle and potentially get to know the Duke of York.

It is also known that during this visit, that Anne contracted the scourge of the seventeenth century: smallpox. Thankfully it seems to have been a mild case of the often deadly virus and she avoided any of the disfiguring scarring that can occur from the accompanying rash. The visit to Paris was cut short when the infant William had taken ill back in the Netherlands. Mary and her household decided it was prudent to return to Orange and the sickly William. It is not known how well James and Anne became acquainted during this visit. However, during the following five years of exile, the pair would have had opportunity to see each other at the various courts visited by Princess Mary.

Shortly after the death of Oliver Cromwell, on 3 September 1658, Anne wrote to her father Edward about the hope of returning to England despite having a position within Mary of Orange's household. The following is taken from that letter:

My Lord,

I received yours of the 1st and am very glad the king is at the frontiers. I pray God this change in England may worke a good one for his majesty and give him cause quickly to come backe that wee might once againe hope to meett in England.

(Clarendon state papers September 1658)

This happiness and hope may well have been at the thought of her life in exile coming to an end and being back with her family, with whom she had maintained correspondence during her time at the court in Orange. However, given that she was a commoner and that she would be married to James, Duke of York, in less than two years from this time Anne Hyde may well have been looking forward to the Duke of York returning to his brother court and becoming better acquainted with him.

Given their difference in status, why would a duke, who was the brother to a king with no kingdom, and in desperate need of a good alliance, marry an English commoner? Firstly it is said that Anne was 'with ready wit and hereditary talents, a conspicuous figure in the entourage of the Princess of Orange'. (Jesse J.H., *Memories of the Court of England During the Reign of the Stuarts*). There is also the possibility that because of Charles's position, James felt that they would never improve their position and wanted happiness over practicalities. Given how his father had felt on the subject of personal life and that he thought it was a personal matter, not a political matter, James may well have agreed with his father in this line of thought. Likewise, why would Anne Hyde consider the Duke of York? Already some of his less attractive qualities were evident within his personality. However, he was a prince as well as a duke. He was the brother to a king. He had seen action in various military campaigns in Europe during the later years of his exile and had been praised for his bravery and military skill. There is also the fact that he was a Stuart, and he probably was more than able to charm the opposite sex – especially, those he found attractive. All in all, it may very well have just been an old fashioned love story.

According to J.R. Henslowe's book on Anne Hyde, Anne and James were likely to have been secretly engaged to each other by September 1658, hence the Duke of York's refusal of several potential candidates for marriage in the years before he and Anne married. Among the potential brides the Duke of York turned down was Mary Lambert, the only daughter to prominent Parliamentarian General John Lambert. The potential match was hoped to bring the monarchy and parliament together in the aftermath of Oliver Cromwell. Anne had been 'dismissed' by Mary of Orange some time before late 1659. The exact reason for this discharge of her services is unknown, but it is quite probable that Mary had learnt of the clandestine relationship between her brother the Duke of York and her lady in waiting.

The couple had pledged a contract of marriage in November 1659 while still on the continent, in the Dutch port town of Breda where Anne and her family had settled through the years of exile. A contract of marriage in the seventeenth century was a promise of commitment to each other, meaning they considered themselves married and acted as if they were; there were, as far as they were concerned, common law husband and wife.

Although the Princess of Orange may have caught on to the blossoming relationship, it seems Anne's father, Edward, had not. He was so angry that he locked his daughter up in their London home. This did not stop the Duke of York and Anne meeting; they were helped by her ladies maid Ellen Stroud as well as her mother, Lady Frances Hyde. In the end it was King Charles who was able to talk some sense in to the angry Hyde. He had put the facts of the contract made at Breda before bishops and judges who would rule that it was lawful according to the church and the laws of England. The dowager queen, Henrietta Maria, disliked her daughter's former lady in waiting and felt she was not a suitable match for her second son, the Duke of York. The couple exchanged vows on 3 September 1660. The service was conducted by the Duke of York's chaplain, Dr Crowther. It is important to note that at this time the duke was still a practicing Anglican.

By October of 1660, news of the scandalous match had reached the ears of the Restoration's biggest gossip, Samuel Pepys, who made comment upon it in his diary on 7 October 1660.

> All dinner time talking French at me and telling me the story how the Duke of Yorke hath got my Lord Chancellor's daughter with child, and that she doth lay it to him. Discourse concerning what if the Duke should marry her.

Pepys of course did not know that the pair were already married weeks before he gossiped about the news over his dinner in October 1660.

The Duke of York, went on to make a declaration about his marriage to Anne:

> I James Duke of York do testify and declare that after I had for many months sollicted Anne my wife in the way

of Marriage, I was contracted to her on 24th November 1659 at Breda in Brabant and after that tyme and many months before I came to England I lived with her (though with all possible secrecy) as my Wife and after my coming into this Kingdome, And that we might observe all that is enjoyed by the Church of England I married her upon the third of September last in the night between 11 and 12 at Worcester House, My chaplain, Dr Crowther performed that office according as is directed by the Book of Common Prayer the Lord Ossory being then present and giving her in marriage of the truth of all which I do take my corporall oath this 18 February 1661 James. (MS 18740 BM)

Anne gave birth to the first of the couple's eight children on 22 October 1660: Charles Stuart, created Duke of Cambridge; he only lived seven months, dying on 5 May 1661.

As well as being James's first wife, Anne is important as she would influence James on the biggest decision of his life. This decision would affect him well after her own premature death in 1671. The decision in question was to convert to the Roman Catholic faith. Of the two of them, it was Anne Hyde, Duchess of York, who first converted Rome. It was not long after his wife's conversion that James followed her example and he too started taking Catholic instruction from a priest with the view to eventually convert to Rome. This became public knowledge in 1669. For anyone else this would have been a personal spiritual change, but for the Duke of York the change would disrupt the politics of his brother's reign, would later cost him his throne in 1688, and affect the relationship he had with his elder daughters. It would also affect the political landscape of Great Britain, changing the institution and role of the of monarchy; a change that is still enforced to the present today in the twenty-first century.

Anne Hyde, the Duchess of York, therefore did play a big role in James's life, even after her death. Her legacy also lived on in the other children she had with the duke. The other children arrived as follows: Mary – later Mary II, born 1662 and died while joint monarch in 1694; James – Duke of Cambridge, he inherited the title of Cambridge because his older brother Charles had died; born in 1663, he died in 1667; Anne arrived in 1665 – she would later become Queen Anne of Great Britain. Next came another Charles, born in 1666 and given the title of the Duke of Kendal, he died in 1667. Edgar, who inherited the title of Duke of Cambridge from his two older brothers, was born in 1667 and died 1671. Edgar was the couple's last son.

Although the James and Anne were practicing Catholics, their surviving daughters Mary and Anne would both be brought up within the Anglican faith. James and Anne's conversions were not popular within a primarily Protestant parliament, therefore the princesses needed to be brought up in the Protestant faith to address the concerns of the government. James's conversion became less of a threat if his children, who could (and indeed did) inherit the throne, were Anglican Protestants.

Anne, the Duchess of York, was seriously ill just prior to her last pregnancy. She died on 30 March 1671 at St James's Palace, seven weeks after she had given birth. She was only 34 years old. Some historians thing that her death might have been caused by breast cancer.

Had James not kept his word and acknowledged his union with Anne Hyde in 1661, he may not have gone on to convert to Roman Catholicism and both his daughters would not have gone on to become queens of England. The Glorious Revolution of 1688, would not have been required and the British political system would not have become a constitutional monarchy at this point in time. By marrying Anne Hyde, James would change far more than his marital status; he changed his denomination of Christianity, and the political landscape of Great Britain for the better.

The Exclusion Crisis,
Rivalry and Plots

The Exclusion Crisis is the name given to the political storm that surrounded the controversial idea of excluding James, while he was the Duke of York, from the throne due to his Catholic faith. During the seventeenth century religion and politics went together hand in hand, both within the houses of parliament in Westminster as well as down the road in Whitehall within the Restoration court of Charles II.

James, Duke of York, was the royal heir as Charles and his queen, Catherine of Braganza, had failed to produce legitimate heirs to inherit the Stuart throne. Unlike Henry VIII, who had faced a similar crisis during his reign, Charles refused to trade his queen for a different wife to achieve this goal. This was despite the Earl of Shaftesbury, who bravely risked the king's wrath several times by suggesting this idea as an alternative to the policy of Exclusion. This crisis spanned the last three parliaments of Charles II's reign and ended with the dissolution of the Oxford Parliament during the spring of 1681, when Charles, frustrated and at a loss at what else to do to pacify the Exclusionists without giving them what they wanted, dismissed his parliament and did not recall them for the last four years of his reign.

With the benefit of hindsight, some seventeenth-century historians have questioned if the word 'crisis' was in fact an accurate description for these last three parliaments. It is, I believe, too simplistic to say that this is an exaggeration, for at the time Charles, his government ministers and the masses, felt that there was a real threat and it was the Exclusionists who attempted to resolve this fear by politically trying to exclude York from the succession. Charles felt that Exclusion would be a threat to the monarchy; if he allowed parliament to dictate the succession of the Crown – what else would they dictate? The British subjects, as well as the early Whig faction, feared that if a Catholic was allowed to take the throne, this would threaten British liberty, Protestantism and laws. (This was an eerily accurate prediction of what did happen). Both sides were wary of the past and fearful of the future, and as a result of this their judgement of the 'crisis' was possibly more exaggerated than the actual threat. That said, some of those fears did become reality when James inherited Charles's throne in early 1685.

These perceived fears had been inflamed further through recent circumstances, namely the discovery of the so-called 'Popish Plot' in 1678, which increased anti-Catholic feelings and caused suspicion to fall on many leading Catholic MPs and Lords, even resulting in several high profile Catholic convictions. It is understandable why even the thought of the Catholic Duke of York taking throne would have become an important issue to the Exclusionists. Just as the dust had begun to settle after the discovery of the Popish Plot, more fear blossomed when Charles became dangerously ill during the summer of 1679. For ten days at end of the summer, the prospect of a Catholic monarch became very real and gave the Exclusionists the excuse they needed to increase their campaigns to try and exclude James from the succession.

Once Charles had recovered from his illness, he tried to resolve the issue of the rivalry, both personal and political, between the two Jameses. This time both Monmouth and York were sent away. Monmouth would also lose his military posts as well as being banished from England, Ireland and Scotland. this was recorded by Charles Hatton in his Manuscripts:

> The Duke of Monmouth is turned out of all command and banished the three kingdoms. This day he has gone to Windsor to surrender his patents.

> (Hatton, Correspondence of the family of
> Hatton 1601–1704, ed. Thompson E.M.
> 1878 Vol 1 p.194)

York wrote to William of Orange of the disgrace of the Duke of Monmouth:

> Though it may make the Duke of Monmouth ... More popular among the ill men and seditious people will quite dash his foolish hopes that he so vainly pursued. This his Majesty resolved in, upon it being represented to him that it was not reasonable to leave the Duke of Monmouth here, and send me back again to Flanders.

(Dalrymple, *Memoirs of Great Britain and Ireland 1790*, Vol I, pp.328–9)

As the Exclusion Crisis refused to dissipate, in 1679 Charles thought it was prudent to send his brother York into temporary exile so that his presence did not inflame more anti-Catholic feeling and he asked him to leave the country for a while. This must have exasperated York as he was the legal heir to the throne. It must have seemed to him that Charles was favouring his illegitimate son Monmouth over him. James set sail for the Dutch Republic on 3 March 1679 under the pretence of visiting his daughter Mary and her husband, William. In August, York was recalled from his unofficial exile in Europe when Charles fell dangerously ill. York arrived at Windsor Castle on 2 September 1679.

Even before the Duke of York's conversion to Catholicism became public knowledge, the Restoration Court of his brother Charles II had created the impression of a pro-Catholic court. Firstly, Charles had married a Catholic wife, and there were several prominent courtiers close to the king who were openly Catholic in their religious preference. This appearance of being a Catholic-friendly court, was again strengthened in 1670 when Charles entered into the 'secret' Treaty of Dover with the Catholic king, Louis XIV of France. Although it was 'secret', it was suspected that such a treaty existed, especially after the visit of the royal brothers' younger sister,

Henrietta Anne, who was affectionately known as Minette. She was the current Duchess of Orleans and rumoured to be rather close to her brother-in-law, Louis XIV.

The Secret Treaty of Dover was a treaty between England and France in which Charles agreed to change his faith to Catholicism (which he did on his deathbed) to support France militarily in their grievances with the Spanish, and to support them militarily against the Dutch. The treaty was formed of two parts: a 'secret' treaty signed in the summer of 1670 and, in effect, a 'cover-up' treaty signed in December of that year by the members of Cabal. The treaty helps explain why Charles did not want to consider finding an alternative Protestant heir to his throne, instead of his very Catholic brother James. The 'secret' part was of course the dangerous subject of Charles's conversion. Charles was clever by not agreeing to a set date for this part, and may have seen making the Duke of York his heir as his way of fulfilling that agreement to his cousin Louis. By doing this Charles himself could be spared the political upheaval and unrest of openly converting to Rome. In return for these terms Charles would receive a pension from Louis to keep him independent from the ever-difficult parliament.

The exact date of James's conversion to Rome is not known and he was able to keep the matter of his faith relatively private and confined to the Restoration Court until 1673 when the Test Acts required an oath to the Anglican church. Any Catholics unwilling to make this oath could no longer hold political, civil or defence offices. James could have taken the oath and continued to practice his faith privately, however, James being James, refused to do so and as a consequence was forced to resign his post as the Lord High Admiral, something he had been proud of in his adolescent years. By this point it was more than apparent that Charles and his queen, Catherine of Braganza, were unlikely to produce a natural child together so James became a bigger threat to the kingdom's souls as he was, by default, the heir to the thrones. What's worse, he was now a Catholic heir to the thrones!

James further inflamed the Protestant nations' fears in 1673 when he remarried (Anne Hyde had died two years previously). The problem with James's choice of second wife was that she was Catholic and Italian. Born as Maria Beatrice Eleonora Anna Margherita Isabella d'Este, in the Italian city of Modena (the home of balsamic vinegar) Mary of Modena came from an Italian noble family that intermarried well. Her family had married successfully into some of the renaissances most influential families, including the infamous Borgias, Sforzas of Milan, and even the French royal family. James was essentially marrying the Anglican British kingdoms into an old powerful and influential Catholic dynasty. No wonder the Exclusionists started to worry. James and Mary of Modena meet for the first time on the day of their second marriage ceremony on 23 November 1673. One of the ways that James could have eased the political fear of his possible succession would have been to marry a Protestant wife. But James being James, would not make that personal compromise for the greater good.

The first Exclusion Bill was introduced to the lower House of Commons on 11 May 1679 by William Russell, Lord Russell. Ten days later on 21 May, the bill had passed both its first and second reading in the House of Commons. The only way Charles could halt the bill moving to the House of Lords was to prorogue the parliamentary session. He did this on 27 May, before finally dissolving that parliamentary session six weeks later, on 3 July 1673. This was not going to stop Russell, or any of the other Exclusionists, they just saw this as a temporary blip in their exclusion agenda.

The Exclusionists – the politicians who wanted to exclude James from the line of succession, were able to organise themselves and hone their support during the period between the parliamentary sessions. Many of the prominent Exclusionists were members of the 'Green Ribbon Club' – a group of men who held the same views on certain aspects of the days politics and who wore a green ribbon by way of identification. To start with they were mostly men unhappy with Charles II and the Restoration Court and would gather in London's coffeehouses, which were notorious political meeting places. Groups such as the Green Ribbon Club would go on to help form the early blueprints that would become the basis of the first political parties. Parliament was meant to reconvene in October 1679, but Charles, prorogued Parliament again which gave the Exclusionists until October 1680, to recruit MPs to their cause outside of a sitting parliament.

The second Exclusion Parliament started on the 21 October 1680, fifteen months after the last session had been so abruptly stopped. On 15 November, the Earl of Shaftesbury introduced the Exclusion Bill to the House of Lords with an impassioned speech. Shaftesbury was challenged in the Lords by George Savile, Lord Halifax. The exchange was witnessed by two key people: the Duke of Monmouth and the king himself.

In the run up to the debate in the upper house, Charles, with the help of Halifax, had canvassed and petitioned the members of the Lords, seeking support for the Duke of York in order to defeat the Exclusion Bill. The canvassing and debate worked and the bill was defeated in the House of Lords by sixty-three to thirty, and as a bonus Charles had defeated the Exclusionists without having to dissolve Parliament.

The Exclusionists next tactic was to debate how to restrict the royal powers any potential Catholic monarch may have should they inherit the throne. Another point debated by the Lords was whether Charles should set aside his wife, Catherine of Braganza, and remarry. This was a step too far for the king and Charles prorogued parliament again before dissolving both houses on 18 January 1681. The next parliamentary session would be the Oxford Parliament, where Charles would end the political avenue of the policy of Exclusion once and for all. (More details of the Oxford Parliament are in the next chapter.)

After the close of the Oxford Parliament there were a hardcore number of Exclusionists frustrated by their lack of success through Parliament. They were so disheartened that they were prepared to risk their lives in an attempt to achieve their political goal through less than democratic methods. Dangerously, in 1683 they decided to take matters into their own hands and remove both the king and the Duke of York in an assassination plot (which became known as the Rye House Plot), thus leaving the Duke of Monmouth, Charles's eldest illegitimate child, as their puppet monarch.

The Rye House Plot takes it name from the place where the intended assassination would have taken place, a manor house surrounded by a moat located in Hertfordshire. At the time of the plot Rye House was being rented by a former Parliamentarian and supporter of Cromwell, Richard Rumbold. In the lead up to the would-be assassination, Rye House was being prepared with supplies, weapons and men, but Rumbold wanted no part in the plot:

> Both insurrection and assassination were discussed, but Rumbold reportedly 'had no great stomach to an insurrection' and refused to participate in an attempt to assassination unless it occurred on the road between London and Newmarket.

> (Greaves; *Secrets of the Kingdom*, p.139)

Rye House was a good location for the plot because it was away from Tory-held London and remote enough for the plans not to be discovered too quickly and therefore more likely to succeed.

The plotters' aim was to assassinate both Charles and the Duke of York on their way back to Whitehall from attending the races at Newmarket at the beginning of April 1683. The plot was foiled as the royal party had to leave Newmarket a week earlier than planned, due to a major fire within the town of Newmarket. The event of the fire was subsequently reported in the *London Gazette*:

> Newmarket March 23rd. Last night between nine and ten a clock a fire happened here which began in a stable

yard and burn so violently the wind being high, that in a few hours above half the town was laid in ashes. Their majesties removed to earl of Suffolk's house.

(*London Gazette*, March 22 1683 – March 26 1683)

This is qualified further by an extract from the diary of Narcissus Luttrell:

On 22 instant at night between nine and ten a fire happened at the town of Newmarket, which began in a stable by the carelessness of a groom taking tobacco: the wind being high it burnt quiet furiously that it consumed half the town... but his majesties house received no damage.

(Luttrell, Narcissus; *A Brief Historical Relation of State Affairs* Volume 1; Oxford, Oxford University Press: 1857 p.253)

The plot was discovered when one of the plotters, Joshua Keeling, defected and decided to expose the plan to the secretary of state, Sir Leoline Jenkins. In return for informing, Keeling wanted pardon for his part in the planning of the treasonous plot. Eventually, on 12 July 1683, the conspiracy to assassinate the king and his brother became public knowledge. Why Keeling became a turncoat is unknown, but an educated guess would be that he believed the plot would soon be discovered, thus by turning informant he hoped to keep his life.

Two of the plotters, Robert West and Robert Ferguson, later independently claimed that even if all had gone to plan, the plot still would not have been ready as those involved were lacking agreement and on key elements of the plan. Many historians of the period see the Rye House plot as a blueprint for the Monmouth Rebellion of 1685, One man who was involved in both plans was the Earl of Argyll, who would lead the Scottish part of Monmouth's attempt to gain the throne. There was also disharmony between the plotters about what should happen should they succeed. Some of them wanted a return to a republic, while the others wanted there to be a monarch in the form of the Duke of Monmouth or William of Orange. Evidence of this confusion among the plotters can be seen in a letter from Earl of Ormonde to the Earl of Arran, dated 7 July 1683:

> Ever since about midsummer day, we have been satisfied of the truth of the information first given of a design laid for the assassination of the King and Duke and for the raising of a rebellion in England and Scotland and although I make them two designs because it does not appear that all who were in at the rebellion were in for the assassination or privy to it.
>
> (Calendar of manuscripts of the Marquess of Ormonde, new series Vol II, p.65)

As the plot unravelled and men came forward, hoping their confessions would save their necks, others became implicated in the planning of this treasonous act. By 1 June 1683, the government had enough confessions and information to investigate the plot.

William Russell, Lord Russell MP for Bedfordshire, was one of those executed and he would make a bad end in Lincoln's Inn Fields. There is a plaque there today to commemorate his execution, where he was beheaded on 21 July 1683 by Jack Ketch. It was six days shy of the two-year anniversary of Russell's execution that Ketch would botch the execution of the Duke of Monmouth on Tower Hill.

One of the saddest casualties of the failed plot was the Earl of Essex, Arthur Capell. He took his own life by cutting his throat in the Tower of London after he was imprisoned for his involvement at Rye House. By doing this rather than being executed he hoped that his family would still be able to inherit his titles and land. Had he have been executed, the title and lands would have been forfeited to the Crown for his treason.

The Duke of Monmouth also came under suspicion from his father the king and his uncle the Duke of York. It was thanks only to his wife Anne, who begged with his father in a letter of 15 October 1683, that Monmouth escaped with his life:

> Since I am so unhappy as to have no hopes of seeing Your Majestie to ask your leave to deliver this letter to you, I had no other way of putting it into your hands …
> I was the more encouraged to do because he writes to me that, except Your Majestie be resolved on his ruin he is sure he can at this time be serviceable to you, so I hope Your Majestie will not refuse to accept of that entire submission and great penitence from him, which your goodness would not perhaps deny to another man. I beg your Majesty will not be displeased with me since I doubt not but that his letter is of consequence because he pressed me deliver it with all speed to Your Majestie.

(Calendar of State Papers Charles II dom
series October 1683 – April 1684, p.35)

Consequently, Monmouth was sent into exile. The damage had been done; Monmouth's relationship with his father changed from this point, and he was no longer Charles's favoured and cherished first born. Monmouth had never been a favourite of his uncle James and his possible involvement with the Rye House Plot would only have sealed James's dislike towards his nephew – a dislike that would eventually set Monmouth firmly on the road to Tower Hill and losing his head.

Monmouth found himself in The Hague and as the guest of his cousins William and Mary. His exile was hardly punishing as he was given a comfortable house and was royally entertained at balls and parties. He even had the company of his long-term mistress Henrietta Maria Wentworth to help him through his exile. Unsurprisingly the Duke of York became angry with his daughter and son-in-law for making Monmouth so comfortable during his exile:

> And let the prince flatter himself as he pleases, the Duke of Monmouth will do his part to have a push with him for the crown, if he, the Duke of Monmouth outlive the king and me ... it will become you very well to speak to him [William] of it.

(Dalrymple; Memoirs of Great Britain and Ireland 1790 Volume III, p.57)

In the aftermath of the discovery of the plot, there is no denying that the safety of the king and his heir had been threatened and there was a fear of civil unrest. The law had to be upheld and Charles had to make examples of the men involved to prevent to future political plotters. It is a shame that the Duke of Monmouth didn't take note, or comprehend how lucky he was to have escaped a worse punishment than exile.

As a result of the Rye House plot and to distract the Exclusionists from focusing on James, Charles decided to send his brother, to Scotland, to perform some of the duties that he as king should have undertaken. This included dealing with the Scottish parliament and ratifying new laws. One of the more ceremonial roles undertaken by the Duke of York was to head up a procession of nobles and MPs in Edinburgh along the royal mile up to parliament. James's official title was that of High Commissioner of the Parliament and he had vice regal authority and power acting as Charles's proxy. It was in this role of proxy for his brother that James was at his most politically successful in dealing with one of his future parliaments. Had he been this accommodating and flexible after 1685 when he was king, in Scotland as well as in England, the Glorious Revolution may not have been needed.

The Exclusionists and their agenda to prevent the Catholic Duke of York from inheriting the throne had changed; they were undoubtedly men ahead of their time with their ideas on democracy, politics and the role of the monarch. These ideas would became reality in 1688 when William and Mary took the throne as constitutional monarchs; a political system still in place in twenty-first century Britain. (See the chapter on the Glorious Revolution)

It is worth examining the animosity between the two Jameses, York and Monmouth, which had been building for many years and came to a head in 1683 with the discovery of the Rye House Plot. After the Restoration, Monmouth had arrived at court as a teenager and the two dukes lived cheek by jowl within Charles's libertine court, and did not get on:

> There is one thing troubles me and puts odd thoughts in my head; it is that all this while his Majesty has never said a word, nor gone about to make a good understanding between me and the Duke of Monmouth, for though it is a thing I shall never seek, yet methinks it is what his majesty might please.
>
> (ref to Darmouth MS; Watson, J.P., Chief General & Rebel Chief pp.110–11)

This sums up the reality of the relationship between the two James and how it probably hurt Charles.

Restoration gossip, courtier and diarist, Samuel Pepys also observed the following of the relationship between the three royals in his diary on 26 July 1665:

> The King having dined, he came down and I went in the barge with him, I sitting at the door hearing him and the Duke [York] talk … they are both princes of great nobleness and spirits. […] The Duke of Monmouth is

most skittish, leaping gallant that ever I saw, always in action, vaulting or leaping or clambering.

The two Dukes did learn to tolerate each other and served together during the second Anglo Dutch war in 1665, when a 16-year-old Monmouth served in the navy under his uncle York, who was the Admiral of the Royal Navy. They were on the flagship, the *Royal Charles* together. It while they were at sea that, on 3 June 1665, Monmouth witnessed and experienced his first Naval battle off the coast at Lowestoft.

The rivalry between the two dukes finally came to a climax after the death of Charles when Monmouth attempted to take the throne from his uncle in what became known as the Monmouth Rebellion (See chapter on the Monmouth Rebellion). It also is symbolic of the political and religious division at court and in Parliament over the issue of a Catholic potentially inheriting the thrones of Great Britain.

* * *

This chapter highlights several important issues in relation to James II the king, why he was disliked and would lose the throne, becoming the last Catholic King of England and Great Britain. First, even before Charles died and York inherited the crown, he was not wanted as king, because he was openly Catholic. Measures both political and treasonous were taken to remove York from the succession in favour of either Monmouth or William of Orange. The rivalry between York and Monmouth is symbolic of the struggle between Catholicism and Protestantism, which would play out in 1685 during Monmouth's rebellion. Lastly, we see political ideas for William of Orange to be heir and monarch as early as 1681, seven years before the events of the Glorious Revolution and James II losing his thrones.

The End of the Restoration Reign
1681–1685

In August 1679 King Charles became dangerously ill and temporarily worried the court, the members of the fledgling Whig and Tory parties, and highlight the fact he had no legitimate heirs of his own, leaving the worrying prospect of his Catholic brother inheriting the throne. Until late August, Charles II had spent a relaxing summer at Windsor, fishing on the River Thames at Datchet, sometimes accompanied by his favourite mistress, the former actress Nell Gwenn – Charles had installed her in a house close to the castle. With parliament dissolved and the Privy Council adjourned for the summer, Charles had very little to worry about apart from being a merry monarch.

Until this point, the 49-year-old monarch had been in fine health. He was known for his love of sport, and regularly played tennis, fenced and took daily constitutional walks with his beloved pet spaniels. Nothing seemed unusual, until the king contracted a cold after a trip to the south coast. On 23 August, the cold became more serious when his temperature rose to a high fever. Over the next few days the symptoms developed into excessive sweating, vomiting, a severe thirst and an inability to pass water. The doctors called to treat the king used the seventeenth-century cure-all of leeching, in the hope that it would help alleviate the illness.

The Duke of Monmouth had been part of his father's court at the time that Charles took ill and was on hand throughout the king's illness, while the Duke of York was still on the continent in exile, oblivious to the king's change in health. Monmouth was also incidentally the most senior courtier at Windsor and had the duty of communicating his father's illness, to the Lord Mayor of London.

The Earl of Sunderland, however, clearly thought that Monmouth should also have communicated the situation to the Duke of York as well as the Lord Mayor of London. In fact, he felt so strongly that Sunderland took it upon himself to write to York himself inform him of his brother's illness. As soon as York received the letter on the 28 August, he packed his bags and returned to court.

As Sunderland's letter was heading to Europe, the king's conditions seemed to deteriorate even further as he developed seizures and fits and lost control of his bowels. It was bad enough that Charles was so dangerously ill, but he was not even given the peace and privacy in which to recuperate. He had no less than seven quack 'doctors' constantly poking and prodding him, half the Privy Council had come to court after hearing of the king's illness, and on top of that his usual servants and gentlemen of the bedchamber were also present.

Thankfully, this illness was short lived, lasting just over a week. By the time the Duke of York had returned to court after three days of hard travel over land and sea, and in a fearful state of worry about his brother, returned to find the king dressed and waiting for his barber to groom him.

This episode is important as it was a wake up call to both Charles and James over the contentious issue of the line of succession. Politically, it reawakened anti-Catholic feeling and forced Charles to decide how to deal with the Exclusionists once and for all.

* * *

Charles's solution to deal with the frustrating and persistent Exclusionists was to shut down the legal and political avenue for them to attack and block the Duke of York as the next in line to he throne. To do this he needed to know what he wanted, to categorically spell out his wishes to the Exclusionists and then close parliament down for the rest of his reign. He knew that this was a risky move and it was mirroring some of his father's autocratic behaviours, but it was a risk he was willing to take. Due to the Treaty of Dover with Louis XIV Charles was financially independent he did not need a parliament – it was a neat solution to a troublesome problem.

He decided to take the last session of parliament away from Westminster and the Exclusionist and Whig stronghold of London and Westminster, and instead hold government in the loyal Royalist university city of Oxford during the middle of March 1681. The full parliamentary session lasted a week, starting on 21 March and closing on the 28th of the same month.

Charles addressed both the houses of his parliament with one of the most eloquent speeches of his entire reign:

> If is as much My Interest, and shall be as much My Care as yours, to preserve the Liberty of the Subject, because the C [...] never be safe when that is in danger. And I would have you likewise be convinc'd, that neither your Liberties nor Properties can subsist long, when the just Rights and Prerogatives of the Crown are invaded, or the Honour of the Govern [...] brought low, and into Disreputation.

The king referred to why the stability of the nation was important for both Crown and government alike, Charles went on to say how he did not dislike his parliament. This was despite his actions, which were taken in frustration. Maybe this was Charles's attempt of demonstrating to parliament and to history that he was not autocratic like his father in regards to his relationship with his parliament:

> I let you see by My calling this Parliament so soon, that no Irregularities in Parliaments shall make Me out of Love with Them; and by this Means offer you another Opportunity of providing for Our Security here, by giving that Countenance and Protection to our neighbours and allies.

Charles goes on to reiterate his position on the succession of his throne in the following extract from his speech:

> What I have formerly, and so often declared touching the Succession, I cannot depart from. But to remove all reasonable Fears that may arise from the possibility of a Popish Successor's coming to the Crown, if means can be found, that, in such a Case, the Administration of the Government may remain in Protestant Hands, I shall be ready to hearken to any such Expedient, by which the Religion might be Preserv'd, and the Monarchy not destroy'd.
>
> I must therefore earnestly recommend to you, to provide for the Religion and the Government together, with regard to one another, because they support each other: And let Us be united at home, that We may recover the Esteem and Consideration We used to have abroad.
>
> I conclude with this one Advice to you, That the Rules and Measures of all your Votes, may be the known and established Laws of the Land, which neither can, nor ought to be departed from, nor ch [...]ng'd, but by Act of Parliament: And I may the more feas [...]bly require, That you make the Laws of the Land your Rule, because I am resolv'd they shall be Mine.

Charles therefore had the last say on the issue of Exclusion. With the Exclusionist and Country faction defeated in Oxford, the Court faction would regain control of London through the election of the Sheriff of London in the July 1682. Soon afterwards, Shaftesbury left England for a self-imposed exile where he died in early 1683. With no strong leadership left and all the legal and political avenues to achieve Exclusion concluded, treason was the only avenue open for the Exclusionists.

* * *

Following the Oxford Parliament of 1681, Charles enjoyed just over three years of his reign at his various courts, including Whitehall and Windsor, with his mistresses and his wife the queen. He indulged in fishing, fencing, tennis, walking his dogs, playing cards, watching plays and entertainments as well as eating well and being merry. On the surface he was healthy and still relatively young for a seventeenth-century man.

This all changed in early 1685 when King Charles II's final illness started. On 1 February the royal court was at Whitehall Palace in London. When the king awoke that morning he decided, unusually, not to take a morning walk with his dogs but to take a carriage ride. The rest of his day passed relatively normally ending in an evening of gambling in the royal rooms of one of his favourite mistresses, Louise de Kérouaille, the Duchess of Portsmouth. The evening was opulent and jolly.

The king had a bad night, which was particularly unusual as he was known to be a good. Upon waking on the morning of 2 February he was visibly and physically ill. His complexion was ashen and during that bad night of unrest he had lost his capacity to speak cohesively and had begun to have fits. Unsure what to do, the gentlemen of the bedchambers started to get Charles ready for the day despite the fact he was clearly seriously ill. It was only when he collapsed in the barber's chair while being shaved that they finally called the royal doctors to attend him. The rest of his day was spent being given all manner of seventeenth-century 'medical' remedies, including bleeding, enemas and cupping. The seriousness of the situation was realised and James as well as the Privy Council were informed and summoned to the king's chamber. James was in such a state of worry that he had only put one shoe on, the other foot was still in its bedtime slipper when he arrived and his brother's side. As the day went on Charles was able to regain cohesive speech and he requested to see his wife, the queen.

Even though Charles was still alive, the city of London were preparing for the inevitable and the officials and dignitaries of the city started to send the Duke of York letters and messages of loyalty and support as the heir to the throne. One can only hope that Charles was not made aware of these messages. Another result of the king's illness was that all of the kingdom's ports were closed and there was a visible increase in security and guards around the court. These measures were so that no news could leave the country and reach the king's eldest son Monmouth, or his host in exile William Prince of Orange. James and the Privy Council thought there was a real risk that one or other of them might attempt to take advantage of the king's illness and possible death, given that the last political crisis of Charles's reign had been the Exclusionists and their cause. There was one exception, as a solitary messenger was deployed to bring news of Charles's illness to his cousin, Louis XIV at Versailles.

The following few days followed a pattern of Charles rallying and seeming better, followed by a swift decline into illness again. He continued to have episodes of fits and periods of disoriented and uncoordinated speech. Again more painful and useless administrations were made by the royal doctors in the hope that he would recover like he had in the summer of 1679. Sadly it was all to no avail.

The king's final day dawned on Friday 6 February 1685. During his final hours he had his brother join him. Even before he had died, the queen was so taken with grief and sorrow that she needed to be helped back to her rooms. Although Charles and Catherine were never passionate lovers they had over the years grown fond of each other, loving each other in the way brothers and sisters love each other.

The most significant thing to happen on Charles's deathbed was his conversion to the Catholic faith, something he felt he was unable to do during his reign. Whether this was a strong personal conviction, or to pacify Louis and the terms of the Secret Treaty of Dover, we can not know. It is however symbolic of just how different the royal brothers of Charles and James were in personality. Charles had chosen his responsibility as head of the Anglican church, over his personal faith or preference while he was a king, unlike his younger brother James who chose his personal spiritual needs over those of the people he was likely to rule by converting to Rome while heir to the throne. And this is the crux of why Charles was able to die as king and in his bed, and why James was unable to maintain the throne and would die in exile.

Charles II died aged 54 years old, surrounded by his courtiers and doctors just before midday on 6 February 1685. The next stage of James's life was about to begin as the last Catholic king of Great Britain and Ireland.

PART 2

James II & VII
&
The Exile Years
1685–1701

The Monmouth Rebellion and The Bloody Assizes 1685

In 1660, at the time of the Restoration I don't think anyone imagined that twenty-five years later the Duke of York would have inherited the throne and re-established a Catholic monarchy, throwing the Protestant nation into a collective state of worry for the future of their souls.

At the time of his father's death, James Scot, Duke of Monmouth, had been enjoying the hospitality of his cousins, William of Orange III and Princess Mary, at The Hague. The horrible task of telling Monmouth that Charles had died fell to William. It is said that Monmouth's cries of grief could be heard on the street outside.

Although he was in exile, Monmouth had managed to carve out a new life for himself. He and his mistress, Lady Henrietta Wentworth, had established themselves a household, they were regulars at William and Mary's court and there were a few English and Scottish Protestants also in exile, both voluntarily and legally imposed for their roles within Exclusionist plots such as the Rye House Plot of 1683. Had Charles gone on to live into old age, Monmouth might have lived a contented and happy life with his mistress, soldiering and attending the court of the House of Orange. Fate, sadly, had other plans for both Monmouth and his uncle James.

Less than a week after the death of Charles II, the Calendar of State Papers were predicting that James's wayward and exiled nephew might attempt to displace his uncle for his late father's throne. Although it is inaccurate hearsay being noted in the state papers, it shows the level of worry the new king and his advisor had surrounding Monmouth and his potential threat to their stability.

Feb 10 [1685]: It is reported by some of the dissenting party that the Duke of Monmouth is in the north of Scotland. Some say he is still in Holland and will not come over until an army is ready to receive him and some place of refuge.

(State Papers James II Domestic series,
February – December 1685, p.6)

Within the pages of the Calendar of State Papers it was prophesied two weeks after the death of Charles II, that there would be confrontation between the Duke of Monmouth and the former Duke of York, now King James II; of course the prediction came true, but the outcome was not correct.

They say two Dukes shall fight for the crown of England, which two dukes they term to be the Duke of York now King, the other the Duke of Monmouth and they say that in this battle the Duke of York shall be slain and the crown party totally routed but there shall be several battles fought before this, yet this battle is supposed to be fought in this year eighty five, by which they do propose to themselves that the King will not live long.

(Historical Manuscripts Commission; Calendar of
State Papers Domestic series dating from
February – December 1685; London, 1960, Entry 138; p.30)

The last line of the prophesy could also be interpreted as partially true, as it predicts a short reign of James II. He may have quashed his nephew's rebellion but ultimately the reign of James II & VII would end in abdication in less than four years' time.

Although the rebellion carries Monmouth's name, it was in fact planned to be carried out in two parts, starting in Scotland so that the military focus would be north of the border, to enable Monmouth to invade and start his rebellion on the south coast. The man who would lead the Scottish portion of the insurrection was the disgraced and exiled Archibald Campbell, 9th Earl of Argyll.

Monmouth's reasons for carrying out this rebellion are clear; he held the firm belief – which had been planted, nurtured and encouraged by his fellow Exclusionists – that he, rather than James, was a more suitable king. His first argument was that he was the late king Charles's son, albeit illegitimate. His second point was that he was Protestant like the majority of the England, Wales and Scotland at this time. However, Argyll had very different reasons for wanting to depose James II and see Monmouth in his place. In order to understand why, it is important to understand both the man and his politics.

Argyll was no stranger to plotting and scheming. In 1663, towards the beginning of Charles II's reign, Argyll had been found guilty of treason but had managed to have his sentence reduced and even get his hereditary lands restored to his family. By the summer of 1664, he had even managed to get a position on the Scottish Privy Council. Argyll subsequently remained true and loyal to Charles, and even supported the king in passing the Scottish Succession Act in 1681. This was somewhat ironic as it allowed the Catholic Duke of York the right to succeed his brother to the Scottish throne. Scotland was the ancestral homeland of the Stuart royal family. The point at which Argyll turned from loyal subject to traitor again, was when the English parliament tried to introduce the Scottish Test Act in 1681.

Like the previous Test Acts passed in the English parliament in 1673 and 1678 respectively, the Scottish Test Act of 1681 was introduced in order to uphold and protect Protestantism within the civil service and all men in public office were required to swear an oath. Argyll tried to stop the act being passed within the Scottish parliament, but it succeeded by just seven votes. There were exemptions to the Test Act: the king, and the Duke of York and his subsequent heirs if and when they arrived. It was the exemptions to which the Earl of Argyll objected so strongly; he could not accept that Scotland's subjects had to swear an oath to a religion they already supported, and yet their monarch was not obliged to swear the same oath. And to add insult to injury, that monarch was supposedly the head of the very faith to which he was exempt for swearing an oath. Argyll saw this as a big potential threat to the Protestants of Scotland. Ironically, It had been the then Duke of York who had called this session of the Scottish parliament in the king's name when the Test Act was passed. Argyll subsequently refused to comply with the new act and once again found himself guilty of treason.

In December 1681, he managed to escape from his jail within Edinburgh Castle, and fled into exile in the Protestant territory of the United Provinces. Once safe in exile, the Earl of Argyll started to outline a scheme to invade Scotland with the intent to cause a rebellion in response to his moral outrage regarding the Scottish Test Act.

The Earl of Argyll and the Duke of Monmouth had become acquainted while the Exclusionists were devising and plotting the Rye House Plot; now that they were both in exile in the same place, and they shared the same mutual enemy, it was only a matter of when they would join forces against James II. Argyll believed it would beneficial if the duke carried out a second rebellion the south of England at an agreed point after he (Argyll) had secured the Scottish capital, Edinburgh.

In the months before his father's death, Monmouth, alongside Argyll, had started to plan a joint invasion for a future date. Neither had predicted or expected the immediate death of Charles II. The late king had been only 54 years old at the time of his death in 1685. This age, even by seventeenth-century standards, was still considered reasonably young for a man who maintained an active lifestyle. Charles also had access to a varied diet of fresh food and the best of the limited but emerging new medical profession. The exception to this was a suspected stroke that Charles may suffered in 1679, but he had bounced back from this quickly. During the last weeks leading to his last illness, Charles had been in good health and spirits both mentally and physically, so the subsequent succession of James II & VII to the throne was earlier than expected, meaning that Monmouth and Argyll's schemes had to be drastically brought forward.

Both men knew that for a joint rebellion to have the best chance of being successful, the timings of both landings needed to be well-timed and executed. They decided that the best course of action was for the Earl of Argyll to land in Scotland first. This was to preoccupy and confuse James's army and keep them distracted up in Scotland and away from Monmouth's invasion party. To have the greatest distance to have the best chance, Monmouth decided to attempt to land on the south-west coast of England for the second uprising. If everything went to plan, the Earl of Argyll would have captured and have full control of Edinburgh when Monmouth arrived in the south of England. They also hoped that Monmouth's arrival would encourage smaller insurgencies in England to start, in order to allow Monmouth to move his volunteer supporters towards London.

Prior to his exile by his father, the Duke of Monmouth had undertaken an unofficial royal progress, meeting the common people of England. In a way that James II could never have done, Monmouth mixed with the everyday people, he ate their food, danced with them and was quickly loved by those he met and interacted with. For his grand plan to succeed, Monmouth needed the people who had danced with him and whose food and homemade cider he had shared two years previously to take up arms and fight with and for him. It turns out he had greatly misjudged their level of support. Monmouth also hoped that his arrival would attract support from non-Anglican Protestant dissenters, with the assumption that they also feared that the Catholic James would persecute them as well. However both Monmouth and Argyll failed to remember that such groups as the Quakers were, and still are, pacifists and would not voluntarily take up arms for any cause.

The standard carried by Argyll's supporters in Scotland was inscribed with the motto: 'For God and Religion, Against Poperie,

Tyrrannie, Arbitrary Government and Erastianism.' Argyll and his supporters were not only anti-Catholic but also against the principle of Erastianism (the belief that the state had say over ecclesiastical matters). For Argyll, God was first and the monarch second, and to reflect and preserve the Protestant faith of the people they ruled over. In other words, Argyll opposed everything that the Duke of York represented.

The rushed plans were finalised in Amsterdam during April 1685. However, Argyll and Monmouth disagreed on when to invade: Argyll wanted to attack prior to James II's coronation, due to be held on 23 April – St Georges Day. This unfortunately would have left both parties only days to mobilise, arm, finance, sail and attack. Monmouth, with his military training and experience, disagreed with this course of action. He understood planning was key to their endeavour succeeding.

Monmouth was also at a disadvantage as he did not have access to the same level of the much-needed funds required for such an operation to be successful. Argyll had the advantage of funds as he had been plotting long before he joined forces with Monmouth. Monmouth also knew that even if he had access to the same level of income as Argyll, he would still require more time to give rudimentary military training to supportive volunteers in order for him to have a fighting chance of winning against the well-trained English standing army and topple his uncle from his late father's throne.

Eventually Monmouth was able to persuade Argyll to delay the start of the rebellions, but events still happened faster than Monmouth would have wanted. It is noted in the domestic state papers of James II on 28 April that James learnt that Monmouth had been 'meeting fugitive rebels I Holland' (State Papers James II, Domestic series, Feb–Dec 1685, p.140) By 12 May James wrote to his son-in-law William of Orange that he was vexed 'at the escape of three rebel ships' going on to express his hope that no more would leave Dutch waters. (State Papers James II, Domestic series, Feb–Dec 1685, p.149)

Argyll set sail for his homeland from the safety of the Dutch republic on 2 May 1685. The Duke of Monmouth would set sail for the south-west of England six days after Argyll had sailed to start his uprising. From the south-west, Monmouth needed to take the important cities of Bristol and Gloucester if he was to have a chance of beating his uncle. It was hoped that by taking Bristol and Gloucester he would attract more supporters and increase his limited supplies. He also hoped that London would, after the capture of Bristol and Gloucester, be seized and held in Monmouth's name by the Whigs and any remaining Exclusionists.

The Earl of Argyll's first mistake was to stop at Orkney on 6 May. He and his rebels, were not welcomed. They then continued, without the added support towards the west coast of Scotland, sailing around the northerly tip of the country. The earl and his supporters eventually arrived off the coast of Mull on 11 May. Argyll now needed to recruit some more support and he began this recruitment drive on the Isle of Islay. The Register of the Privy Council of Scotland records a proclamation commanding a levy of Scottish forces to prepare for the impending invasion by the earl:

> Late Earl of Argyll hath not only consulted and concurred with the English conspirators in their late treasonable plot against the King's person … but hath been eminently active … the King being obliged by the law … to established lieutenancies in the shires of Argyll and Tarbet for preventing and suppressing the projects and seditions intended by the said late Archibald.
>
> (The Register of the Privy Council of Scotland,
> Third Series, Volume 10; Edinburgh.
> HM General Register House, 1908–1970, p.327)

Like his co-conspirator Monmouth, the Earl of Argyll grossly over-estimated the level of support he was hoping to attract. He had asked his son to recruit men from their own tenants, but very few tenants complied with their landlord's treasonous call to arms.

The rebels ambitious plans were very reliant on unpredictable factors in an age when communication could take weeks. With hindsight, this is one of the biggest gambles that both Argyll and Monmouth undertook. Another large gamble was Monmouth's ability to attract the same level of the support he had seen on his progresses in 1682 and 1683. The general populace needed to be comfortable to publicly turn against their new king. This misjudgement would be fatal. Monmouth and Argyll had failed to realise that many people were within living memory of the bloody Civil Wars of the 1640s and the deterrent affect it had on them. They ultimately decided that the risk of a potential long-drawn out civil war or charges of treason were not worth the risk of taking up arms for a charming, handsome, Protestant – but illegitimate – duke.

The plan also needed an element of surprise for them to have been at their most effective and both Argyll and Monmouth had lost this. James was able to prepare for both of the invading parties and anticipate what their agendas hoped to achieve. James also made sure to protect London and had a limited time to prepare the troops to defeat both Argyll and Monmouth; for James, like Monmouth, was a military man. Evidence of this can be found in the state papers when James wrote to the Prince of Orange on 22 May 1685, telling his son-in-law of 'Argylls landing in the highlands' (State Papers James II, Domestic series, Feb–Dec 1685, p.175)

The next problem Argyll faced was that he was struggling to keep and maintain discipline among his new recruits. These men were not militarily trained, they were labourers. Lack of focus and boredom left time for fighting, drinking, gambling and eventual desertion. Ironically, the earl had hoped to recruit a large section of his supporters from the Covenanters; the same Presbyterian sect that the Duke of Monmouth had defeated at the Battle of Bothwell Bridge in 1679.

Advanced warning meant that James II had been one step ahead and had taken the precaution of sending loyal Royalist troops to areas where there was the strongest support for the Earl of Argyll cause. As no immediate battle took place, the undisciplined men began to lose faith in Argyll and his cause and began to desert him. The rag-tag army moved from Bute, to Corval in Argyllshire, on to Greenock, before moving to Inveraray. From there, Argyll and his men headed to the garrison of Eileen Gheirrig, before making a temporary base at Ardkinglas Castle. It was not long before they decided to return back to Eileen Gheirrig. By this point, another disaster struck as Argyll had lost the ships he had used to sail to Scotland from Europe. He now had no way of escape – he must have realised that his was now a fight for his life. What is worse is that he had no means of communicating with Monmouth and relaying all that had gone wrong.

With few options left, Argyll headed towards Scotland's second city, Glasgow. At this point, Argyll only had 2,000 men and this soon dwindled further and Argyll found himself left with only a handful of supporters, one of which was his son John. Argyll realised at this point that he was defeated and the men decided to separate to avoid drawing attention to themselves in an attempt to evade capture. This plan was not to succeed.

On 18 June, Argyll was captured by a group of royal militia. His attempt to shoot his captors failed because his gunpowder had become damp. The Scottish rebellion had officially come to an end. Argyll's capture is recorded in this extract from Narcissus Luttrell:

The rebels in Scotland march towards Sterling [sic] …
and attempting to cross the river Clyde, the king's forces
overtook them and dispersed them presently: Argyll
himself was taken.

(Luttrell, N. *A Brief Historical Relation of
State Affairs*, p.348)

Argyll's arrest and those of his fellow rebels can also be found within the Scottish Privy Council papers. On 18 June, Argyll's captor was rewarded £50 for his efforts:

> Argyll is expected as a prisoner and orders are given for his passage to the castle ... the cash keeper to pay John Riddell, £50 sterling for apprehending Argyll.

> (Register of the Privy Council of Scotland, Third Series Volume 11, 20 June 1685, p.x.)

Two days after his capture, Argyll was brought to Edinburgh, questioned and held in prison. He was allowed a visit from both his wife and his sister, Lady Lothian. On 30 June 1685, he was brought to Edinburgh's place of execution, where he faced death by an early form of the guillotine, known by the Scots as the Maiden. He declined to make a final speech, but it is said that on the scaffold Argyll joked, saying that he was about to meet 'the sweetest maiden he had ever kissed. (Willock, J., A *Scots Earl in Covenanting Times*, p.421)

The Duke of Monmouth landed at Lyme Regis, Dorset, on 11 June 1685, with around 150 supporters. Among those he brought with him were his fellow exiles who had escaped punishment after the Rye House Plot, including Lord Ford Grey, Nathaniel Wade and Robert Ferguson. The first of many miscalculations made by Monmouth had became reality within hours of landing when the once popular duke was unable to recruit large numbers of Protestant dissenters to join his cause. Monmouth knew that timing was important however, he did not know that the element of surprise also required for this to work had been lost. His uncle knew of both Argyll's and his invasions and had started planning how to defeat them. With hindsight, the rebellion was always going to be doomed. Just two days after the Duke of Monmouth arrived, James II issued a Proclamation from Whitehall, warning the people of England against his wayward nephew and his treasonous scheme.

Three proclamations one for the seizing of James Duke
of Monmouth and his accomplices; The other for the
suppression of a traitorous declaration published by
the said Duke of Monmouth aforesaid; and the last for
a reward of five thousand pounds for the taking and
securing of his body either dead or alive.

(The Manuscripts of the most Honourable
Marquis of Ormonde New series Vol 7, p.354.)

Although James had known of the planned invasions, this threat must
have given the newly crowned king legitimate reason to be concerned.
James had a national army of 10,000 men, as well as access to local
militia who, although trained, had little or no experience of real
fighting. He needed to keep the militia where each unit was based,
so that if local insurrections broke out they were on the spot to deal
with the problem swiftly. There was the slight risk that James would
face desertions from his trained and well-equipped militia for the
charismatic Monmouth and his Protestant cause, but it was a risk he
needed to take. It must have been a vexing time for such a new and
controversial king.

The Duke of Monmouth's strategy was to march his followers to
Somerset in order to gather more men to join his rag-tag group of
volunteers. Monmouth approached the town of Bridport on 14 June
1685, where he engaged with the local royal militia. At this point,
the Earl of Argyll was still attempting to get to Edinburgh. At this
stage in the rebellion, James and Monmouth were evenly matched
strategically, although there was a significant difference in numbers
and resources. The city of Salisbury was of key importance to this;
if the king's men reached the city, which was roughly six days hard
march from London, it would have been impossible for them to return
to London and prevent the Protestant capital declaring for the Duke of
Monmouth. News of his nephew's arrival reached James on 13 June
and is noted in a letter recorded in the domestic state papers of James II:

Image of James II & VII from 1685, the year he assended the throne of England. Artist Ann Killigrew.

KING JAMES II. LANDING AT KINSALE (*see page* 394).

Above: King James II landing in Kinsale taken from a later book, *British Battles on Land and Sea, volume 1,* from 1873.

Left: Contemporary seventeenth-century picture of James II of England artist unknown.

James as the Duke of York circa 1670,
Artist John Baptist de Medina.

James as Duke of York a year before he ascends the
throne in 1684, Artist Godfrey Kneller.

Prince James, Duke of York 1639, artist
Cornelius Johnson.

A close-up of an infant James Duke of York
taken from a picture of Charles I's children
by Van Dyke, 1635.

Gold Guinea coin from the last months of James II's reign.

A copy of James II's signature.

Left: James II & VII coat of arms.

Below: Father & Son. Charles I and his second eldest son, the future James II. Artist Peter Lely, 1647.

Above: James II in exile after the Glorious revolution with his Wife Mary of Modena and their children. Artist Pierre Minard, 1694.

Below: James II & VII coronation engraving.

Above: 1660, last ball in the Hague before leaving for England and the start of the restoration reign of Charles II. The artist was Hieronymus Janssens, 1660.

Left: James's first wife, Anne Hyde, who was the mother of Queens Mary II and Anne. The portrait dates from 1665, and is by royal artist Peter Lely.

Charles II elder brother to James II. Coronation portrait painted by
John Michael Wright.

Queen Anne, James's second daughter with Anne Hyde, last of the Stuart Monarch. Artist Michael Dahl, 1705.

Above: James Scott, Duke
of Monmouth, leader of
the Monmouth Rebellion,
illegitimate son of Charles II,
and nephew of James II.
Artist Jan Van Wyck, date of
picture unknown.

Right: James Scott,
Duke of Monmouth in
his Garter Robes 1682.
Artist Peter Lely.

William III of Orange and his wife Mary Stuart. William and Mary would succeed the throne from James II in 1688 after the Glorious Revolution. William was James II's son-in-law and nephew and Mary was James II's daughter. This image is taken from the Painted Hall in Greenwich, London, and the artist is Sir James Thornhill.

James Francis Edward Stuart who became known as The Old Pretender and was King James II's controversial Catholic son and heir at the centre of the Warming Pan Scandal of 1688. The artist was Marie-Anne Belle Cheron.

Thomas Osborne, Earl of Danby and Duke of Leeds. He was a prominent figure in the Restoration court of Charles II and would be a leading figure in the Glorious Revolution. The picture is by two artists: Johann Kerseboom and Jan Van der Vaart, dated 1704.

Left: King Louis XIV the Sun
King of France, royal cousin to
James II and his host during his
last years in Exile in France.
the artist was Hyacinthe
Rigaud, circa 1700.

Below: Chateau de Saint
Germain en Laye, the palace
that Louis XIV gave James II
to be his home while in exile.

Mary Stuart, Princess Royal and William II of Orange. This Mary Stuart was the sister to Charles II and James II and the mother of William III of Orange – not to be confused with her niece and daughter-in-law of the same name who would become Queen Mary II. The artist is Gerard Van Honthorst, 1647.

John Churchill, later the Duke of Marlborough, defeated Monmouth at the Battle of Sedgemore in support of James II. However, it was his change of alliance in favour of William and Mary that would contribute to the success of the Glorious Revolution. Artist John Closterman, circa 1685.

James II's parents, Charles I and his wife Henrettia Maria of France. Artist Unknown.

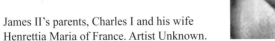

13 June Earl of Sunderland to deputy lieutenant of Cheshire: The king this morning received advice that on Thursday last the Duke of Monmouth with 3 ships a frigate of about 30 guns and 2 small vessels appeared in sight of Lyme, Dorsetshire, landing at night with about 150 men and seizing the town.

(State Papers James II, Domestic series,
February – December 1685, p.193)

Monmouth had both the experience and reputation of being a great military man, which was something James had seen for himself. He must have feared that his nephew had more than a good chance of winning more support to his side and maybe even succeeding in his rebellion and taking the crown from him. As the first few days of the invasion unfolded and James received news of his nemesis' progress.

Monmouth's rebellion was starting to gather pace and his next stratagem was to head towards Axminister. He had managed to gather a volunteer army of approximately 6,000 Protestant Dissenter men, all willing to risk their lives to save the nation from the threat of Rome. From Axminster, he marched his men to Taunton and Monmouth was welcomed to the town like a king.

This area of England were textile and mining communities, and in economic recession at this time. The young, unemployed men were frustrated and needed something or someone to blame for their ill fortune and the rebellion gave them an opportunity to vent their frustrations. It is worth noting that unemployed does not necessarily mean peasant. The records of the 'Bloody Assizes', show that the men who took part in the rebellion were skilled artisans such as weavers, tailors, cobblers, blacksmiths, brewers and yeoman farmers. What the men did not have was any formal military training or experience. (Chandler, D., Sedgemoor 1685, p.8.)

When the duke arrived at Taunton on 20 June, his ships had been taken by the Royal Navy, just off the coast of Lyme Regis. Escape was now unfeasible; Monmouth was now literally fighting for his life. In Taunton, on 21 June 1685, Monmouth was declared 'King Monmouth' by the locals. It is thought up to 7,000 men had joined his cause at this point. But as Monmouth was getting caught up in cries of 'King Monmouth', James II received some good news from Scotland. This is recorded in a letter found in the Domestic series of State Papers. The letter was from the Earl of Sunderland to the Duke of Albermale on the 24 June 1685: 'The king has just received a further account and confirmation of the entire defeat of the rebels in Scotland and the taking of Argyll, who is brought to Edinburgh Castle.'

As Argyll was lost, Monmouth's next goal was the port city of Bristol. To capture this city would make the duke a bigger threat to James II. The king, however, had predicted this manoeuvre and on 17 June, sent orders to the Duke of Beaufort, instructing him to lead the local militias of Hereford, Monmouthshire and Gloucester into Bristol. Also to James's benefit, Monmouth's advance towards Bristol was slowed up by bad weather. The rebels then faced problems crossing the River Avon, as James's troops, aided by the local militia, had either destroyed or heavily guarded the remaining crossings. As Bristol was no longer an option, Monmouth decided to attempt to take Bath. In the hope of a warm welcome, Monmouth sent a messenger ahead of him to the city requesting that the peoples surrender to him and his Protestant cause. Bath answered the duke by shooting the messenger and sending him back to the rebels. The message was clear, people of Bath were loyal to King James II.

Now Monmouth and his men had no choice but to head towards the town of Frome and it was here that he learnt that Argyll had been caught and consequently lost his head. Monmouth knew that he had little option but to keep going on this path and that the odds were now against him. Passage to Frome was also impossible due to Royalist troops, so once again he and his remaining loyal men were forced to change their plans and head towards the cathedral city of Wells. They found that they were low on ammunition and had to resort to plundering the roof of the cathedral for lead in order to make bullets. They further desecrated the cathedral by using the central nave as a stable for their tired and weary horses and animals. For a cause being fought in the name of religion, these actions were not going to win them further support and it was a bad omen.

From Wells, Monmouth and his dwindling number of supporters, travelled towards Bridgwater.

On the evening of 5 July 1685, after twenty-five days roaming around the West Country, the Duke of Monmouth and his men were perilously close, once again, to the royal troops. The king's infantry was being led by John Churchill, the future Duke of Marlborough, and the men were encamped in a small village called Westonzoyland, located on the edge of the plain of Sedgemoor. On the eve of the battle of Sedgemoor, Monmouth's men were ill-prepared for the fight ahead of them. Nothing they had encountered thus far had prepared them for what was about to happen on Sedgemoor plain. They had low ammunition, were largely untrained and many were weary after days of fruitless marching. Some were armed with little more than farming tools, and most of the weapons were either older firearms dating from the Civil Wars, or just basic pikes. On that summer's evening in 1685, Monmouth and Lord Grey climbed the church tower of St Mary's, in order to survey their enemy, and plan their attack.

Monmouth knew that their best chance would be if they attacked under the protective cover of darkness. Early on Monday 6 July 1685, Monmouth led his men to the flat lands of the plains of Sedgemoor. Here the king's troops were encamped. Monmouth's men began their attack from their base in Bridgwater. After half a mile, the duke's men started across the moorland under the early morning darkness. Visibility was hampered due to fog, making crossing the marshy terrain hazardous. Through luck more than anything else, the rebels got several miles without being detected by the royal troops.

This lasted until they needed to cross the Longmoor Rhyne, a ditch that crossed the moorland. This drainage ditch was roughly a mile from the site where the battle would take place. The first piece of bad luck was when a pistol was accidentally let off. The noise started the farm horses commandeered by the duke. These animals were useless in the battle as the noise of the fighting soon caused them to flee in terror – with or without their riders. This had been another oversight by Monmouth, and to make matter worse the duke's men had now lost their element of surprise.

There was no other choice but to start fighting. Grey led the remaining mounted men towards the king's cavalry. The duke's musketeers and pikemen now found themselves at a disadvantage as their old weaponry hindered the fight further. During the opening engagements of the battle, when the dawn had not fully broken and foggy mists blurred vision, both sides needed to try and recognise their enemy. The most efficient way was by asking figures in the near distance who they were fighting for. The duke's men would respond, 'King Monmouth! King Monmouth!' and 'God with Us!' The latter cry was used by the Cromwellian forces during the Civil Wars. Monmouth attempted leading his rag-tag army in the battle by shouting orders, however his words were not heard in the mêlée. The lack of training, equipment and preparation, along with poor discipline among his volunteers would, be Monmouth's Achilles heel.

In contrast, as Monmouth struggled, Churchill's well-trained and disciplined militia, who had access to a good supply of ammunition and up-to-date weaponry were holding their own in the fight. It was the use of cannon by the king's men that would bring the unfair battle to an end. Those rebels not killed by the weapon's blast, ran in fear of it.

Upon entering the battle, Monmouth was thought to have had 4,000 volunteers. That was 1,000 more men than the royal opposition. An hour and a half of bloody fighting would leave 1,300 of the duke's men dead, compared to only 200 royal lives lost. Unfortunately, for

Monmouth's volunteers, the death toll did not stop after the battle. A further 320 men would face execution for their part in his treason. Another 750 souls would be transported for hard labour for their part in the rebellion.

The Battle of Sedgemoor had lasted little over ninety minutes. Monmouth knew that the rebellion was over and his high stakes gamble had not paid off; he was a traitor on the run from his uncle the king. News of the duke's defeat travelled swiftly; the Dean of Wells Cathedral is recorded as saying: 'The intervening 6 July, auspicious day! Brought an end to the rebellion and downfall to the rebels at Weston Zoyland in this county!' (Calendar of Manuscripts of the Dean and Chapter of Wells, Vol 2, p.448). There is little wonder that the Dean of the cathedral was happy upon hearing of Monmouth's defeat. If this was the response from a man of the cloth, the Duke of Monmouth could hardly expect compassion from the uncle against whom he had plotted.

Monmouth, along with his friend and fellow commander, Lord Grey, changed their clothes to look like peasant farmers. They hoped to reach the coastal town of Poole, to catch a ship towards mainland Europe. Unfortunately for them they would never reach the town of Poole. After two nights sleeping rough in ditches and hedgerows, the two friends separated on the 7 July. Lord Grey was the first of the two to be detained. He was found in the New Forest town of Ringwood, only 16.5 miles from Poole. The following day, the Duke of Monmouth was discovered sleeping in a hedge. After the two men's arrest, the *London Gazette* published the following royal proclamation:

> His Majesty has been pleased to cause his Royal Proclamation to be published for a solemn and publick thanksgiving throughout the kingdom for his majesties late victories over the rebels

(*London Gazette*, 9–13 July 1685)

The two comrades and friends were reunited when they were held for two nights in Ringwood before going on to London to await their different fates. Monmouth only made one request at Ringwood; he asked to be given paper, pen and ink.

The journey from Dorset to London took four days and was very heavily guarded to dissuade Whig fanatics from attempting to rescue the duke. During the journey, Monmouth was melancholic in mood. By comparison, Lord Grey was said to have been positive about their situation. On 13 July, a week after they were defeated, the two men reached London. Upon their arrival, the prisoners were transferred from their guarded carriage to waiting barges. They were then taken to the Palace of Whitehall for an audience with James II and to discover their fates. Even before Monmouth had arrived in London, James had started arranging his nephew's execution. On 12 July he sent the following memorandum to the keeper of the Great Seal to prepare for the event:

> James late Duke of Monmouth, has been attainted by an Act of Parliament made in this present parliament … and thereupon stands attained of high treason and is to suffer the pains of death as a traitor … the said late Duke is now a prisoner at the King's will and pleasure; and … Commanding them to receive the body of the said late Duke and forthwith to cause execution of him to be done … forthwith to bring him to the scaffold upon the Tower Hill and then there cause his head to be cut and stricken off clearly severed from his body and this execution to be on Wednesday next the 15.

(Calendar of State Papers Domestic series dating from State Papers Domestic, February – December 1685, p.259.)

James did grant Monmouth an audience, but as can be seen above, the outcome of that meeting was not going to be changed. The meeting was probably agreed to so that James could give the duke his sentence in person. It is also not unreasonable to assume, given James's personality and dislike towards his nephew, that he probably wanted to gloat over his victory. We have seen that James II was a vain, petty and meanspirited, and this would not have been beneath him. The exchange between uncle and nephew is briefly mentioned within the Calendar of State Papers, but it does not give the details of what passed between the two men. What happened in Whitehall stayed in Whitehall. The only source of the meeting was recorded by Sir John Dalrymple in his memoir:

> The Duke of Monmouth seemed more concerned and desirous to live and did behave himself not so well as I expected nor so as one ought to have expected from one who had taken upon him to be King. I have signed his death warrant for his execution tomorrow.
>
> (Dalrymple; *Memoirs of Great Britain and Ireland 1790*, p.134.)

Monmouth did not legally require a trial as parliament had already passed an Act of Attainder. The attainder declared that the Duke of Monmouth had been found guilty by parliament of High Treason; the only thing that could have saved his life would have been a royal pardon.

One can only imagine what, in a desperate and last-ditch attempt to save himself, the doomed Duke of Monmouth might have done in the presence of his uncle, James. He was never able to foresee the consequences of his actions. His father, Charles II, had always excused his son or bailed him out of whatever dangerous or misguided mess he had gotten himself embroiled in. This time, James, Duke of Monmouth's, luck had run out.

Monmouth was left to consider his fate in the Tower of London. James was not completely hard-hearted, as he did allow Monmouth concessions. He was permitted to have a servant and was granted an audience with his wife and children on the morning of his execution upon Tower Hill. (Calendar of State Papers James II, Domestic series, Feb-Dec 1685, Entry 1221, p.261) Anne, the duke's long-suffering wife, and his neglected children came to visit him. The duchess's behaviour was very gracious, especially considering his appalling behaviour towards her. She asked for his forgiveness and he begged her pardon in return, before turning to his children to say his final goodbyes.

At 10 am on 15 July 1685, the Duke of Monmouth left the Tower of London. The keeper of the Tower handed him over to the sheriffs of London. They in turn took him the short distance to the scaffold, especially erected upon Tower Hill for the purpose of his execution. Unfortunately for the duke, the man tasked with the job was the infamous, and notoriously bad, executioner Jack Ketch, who had so ineptly dispatched Monmouth's friend Lord Russell in July 1683.

Monmouth set about putting his affairs in order and his main worry during his last days and hours seems to have been for the reputation and welfare of his true love, Lady Henrietta Wentworth. Even on the scaffold only moments before he took his leave of the world, Monmouth tried to restore Henrietta's reputation:

> I confess I lived many years by all sorts of debauchery. But Since that time I had an affection for the Lady Harriot [Henrietta] and I prayed that if were pleasing to God, it might continue, otherwise that it might cease. And God heard my prayer.
>
> (Eachard L, History of England p.1060)

These words are a tragic yet beautiful declaration of love for a woman who had been so important to Monmouth in the later part of his life.

How many of us would be able to think of another like that, knowing that we were about to die in such circumstances?

The Duke of Monmouth's death was also recorded in the following extract taken from Narcissus Luttrell's history of the period:

> The late Duke of Monmouth on the 15, he was accordingly that day brought from the Tower to a scaffold on Tower Hill … He was habited in a grey cloth suit … he gave a paper to the Bishops and declared himself for the Church of England: he was very composed. After near an hour he laid himself down and the executioner did his office, but had five blows before he sever'd his head … there was no shouting but many cried: this done his body and head were put into a coffin covered in velvet and carried back to the Tower where after were buried.

> (Luttrell, N., *A Brief Historical Relation of State Affairs*, pp.353-4.)

Traditionally, the bodies of traitors executed for High Treason, were tarred and left on display on London Bridge as a warning to others. James spared his nephew this final humiliation, most probably for the sake of his late brother. James, late Duke of Monmouth, was laid to rest in the Tower of London's chapel of St Peter ad Vincula. He still lies in that chapel, resting for all eternity, in a grave situated under the altar.

In a letter to William of Orange, James II said of Monmouth's death: 'He died resolutely and a downright enthusiast.' (Dalrymple; *Memoirs of Great Britain and Ireland 1790*; James's letter to William of Orange, 17 July 1685, p.135.) Monmouth's death was also recorded in the diary of John Evelyn: 'darling of his father and the ladies … debauch'd by lusts, seduc'd by crafty knaves … he failed and perished.' (Evelyn, J., Diary, 15 July 1685) Evelyn's words sum up how I feel about James Scott, late Duke of Monmouth; he was spoiled and easily led.

The consequences for those who had become embroiled in the duke's schemes in the West Country were about to be avenged by King James. Six weeks after Monmouth was executed on Tower Hill, the commoners who had been involved were sent to trial at the local assizes, the first of which was held in Winchester. Their trials were heard by Lord Chief Justice, Judge George Jeffreys. He was joined by a further four judges to try the 1,000 plus people accused of helping Monmouth. The other judges in attendance were: Sir William Montague, Sir Robert Wright, Sir Henry Pollexfen and Sir Creswell Levinz.

The judges travelled to Salisbury, Dorchester, Exeter, Taunton and Wells before all those accused were finally tried. It is thought about 1,400 faced the judges. Taunton was the worst place for executions when 144 convicted souls were executed in just two days between September 17 and 19, their bodies left on display in the town as a warning to the residents. About 850 were deported to the Caribbean to undertake hard labour for their crimes. Many died while waiting for their judgement in the poor conditions of seventeenth-century jails. 'Gaol fever', the cause attributed to these deaths, is widely thought to be typhus – some may think this was a mercy compared to facing the handguns, rope or years of hard labour. Among those executed was the last woman to be burnt alive in England, Elizabeth Gaunt.

Jefferys's harsh punishments would lead these trials to become known as 'The Bloody Assizes'. Given that the country was fearful of a tyrannical king, James could have used these trials to show that he was a merciful king in his treatment of locals who became embroiled in Monmouth's plans. Instead, he acted just as they feared he would do.

The harsh Judge Jeffreys would become known to history in an equally unflattering manner by being given the nickname of the 'Hanging Judge'. Fate did not treat him well either. In the early days of the Glorious Revolution at the end of 1688, the Hanging Judge found himself incarcerated, in London's most notorious gaol, The Tower of London. He did not last long, dying on 18 April 1689. He had a pre-existing health issue with his kidneys; being imprisoned exacerbated the problem, causing him to die of kidney disease.

This episode early in James II's reign helped to solidify Protestant fears surrounding him as a Catholic monarch. He lost the opportunity to prove that he was compassionate and instead indulged in proving his authority as king. It would set the tone of the next three years of his short reign.

The Glorious Revolution of 1688

By the autumn of 1688, James II & VII had managed to isolate himself and turn a substantial number of MPs, landed gentry and the populace at large, against him. Those who had been staying loyal to the king because he had no Catholic heir finally abandoned him at the arrival of a son, James Francis Edward. James's reign would no longer be a Catholic interlude, but the start of a Catholic dynasty over a predominantly non-Catholic nation. The potential political, social and religious upheaval, both domestically and internationally, lay heavy in the minds of his subjects; many of whom were still within living memory of the bitter Civil Wars of James's father, Charles I.

When James inherited the throne in 1685, it could be argued that because he had no living legitimate male heir from his Catholic marriage to Mary of Modena, people where less worried about the future of the Church of England. His two surviving daughters from his first marriage, who would potentially inherit the throne, were both Protestant and married to Protestant husbands. In theory, therefore, because James II was 52 years old when he came to the throne, his reign was expected to be short.

This may also have been one of the reasons why the Duke of Monmouth received less support than he had expected for his ill-fated rebellion in the summer of 1685. Although he was Protestant, the people of England and Scotland preferred to back the legitimate king with no heir, than risk a potential Civil War.

This feeling of uncomfortable acceptance by the Anglican Protestants of James's government would turn into alarm in late 1687, when the queen, Mary of Modena, fell pregnant. The subsequent birth of Prince James Francis Edward Stuart, on 10 June 1688 would change the course of British history, as well as the lives of his father and half sisters, Mary and Anne. This royal birth had the potential, should the prince survive past infancy, to create a Catholic dynasty upon the British throne. Instead his birth would become the trigger for events that would modernise the political landscape of Great Britain and bring about one of the strangest conspiracy theories of British history: the scandal of the warming pan.

When things seemed to be going in James's favour he was never able to let things run their course. Instead the king could not help upsetting the applecart during the months leading to the birth of his son in 1688. During April of that year, when Mary of Modena's pregnancy was more secure, James decided to upset his precarious relationship with the Anglican church. He did this by insisting that a Declaration of Indulgence be read on 27 April during Sunday services. During the year before, James had previously issued the same Declaration, but it had not been welcomed by the Church of England. The Declaration of Indulgence was a statement that aimed to attempted to stop civil and religious restrictions against the Catholic minority in Britain. So it is easy to understand why the Protestant establishment worried when they heard the content of the indulgence. Secondly, he is indiscreetly implying in a Protestant service that if he has a son, he will be Catholic as well as his heir. What really makes this move insensitive is that although James II was Catholic himself, he was still the head of the Anglican church within England. The Anglian communion felt threatened by the Indulgence as they feared it would not only allow Catholics freedom to worship, but other faiths too such as Judaism, Islam or Hinduism:

> we have resolved to use our utmost endeavours to establish liberty of conscience on such just and equal foundation as will render it unalterable, and secure to all people the free exercise of their religion for ever, by which future ages may reap the benefit of what is so undoubtedly for the general good of the whole kingdom.

97

It is such a security we desire, without the burden and constraint of oaths and tests, which have been unhappily made by some governments ... We must conclude, that not only good Christians will join in this, but whoever is concerned for the increase of the wealth and power of this nation.

(Declaration of Indulgence,
James II & VII 27 April 1688)

The hierarchy of the Anglican communion refused to read the king's reissued Indulgence as he commanded in April 1688. It was at this point that seven of England leading bishops decided that they needed to approach the king about his declaration. These rebellious clergy were: William Sancroft, Archbishop of Canterbury; John Lake, Bishop of Chichester; Thomas Ken, Bishop of Bath & Wells; Jonathan Trelawney, Bishop of Bristol; William Lloyd, Bishop of St Asaph; Thomas White, Bishop of Peterborough; and Francis Turner, Bishop of Ely. They came together to contest the reading of the declaration to their congregations citing that the declaration had been drawn up in an undemocratic way using autocratic royal authority, not through the recognised elected parliament. At the time of the reissue of the Indulgence, James had dismissed both of his parliamentary houses. The clergy therefore argued that the declaration was illegal. Not unsurprisingly James did not agree, and after they had raised their legitimate concerns with their monarch, the archbishop and six bishops were arrested on the charges of sedition and libel. They were subsequently imprisoned in the infamous Tower of London. All seven clergymen were tried and found not guilty of both charges on 30 June 1688.

The symbolism and timing of such a statement was not lost on the political watchers of the time. James was attempting to overturn the Test Acts of 1673 and 1678 by his command in an autocratic fashion, rather than through parliament. James had personally lost out due to the Test Act, being forced to resign his post as Lord High Admiral of the Royal Navy. For him this was not just political, it was personal. This kind of behaviour was highly reminiscent of James's late father, King Charles I, and of his Catholic royal cousin, Louis XIV of France.

The fallout of this unfortunate episode was that James was displaying worrying displays of behaving just like his late father, Charles I. People worried about the potential consequences of their king behaving in this autocratic manner. The nature of the Declaration of Indulgence also caused increased social anxiety as it looked like James was attempting to convert England and Scotland to Roman Catholicism through the Anglican pulpit. This behaviour resurrected the dormant ghost of the Exclusionists, the anti-Catholic movement started during Charles II's reign. The Exclusionists were largely early Whigs, who were predominantly Protestant and had hoped to exclude the Catholic James from the throne in favour of either the Duke of Monmouth, Charles's eldest illegitimate and Protestant son, or the Protestant William of Orange, who was both Charles's and James's nephew, as well as James's son-in-law. Unlike the original Exclusionists, these new anti-Catholic statesmen started to work out how to depose Catholic James and restore Protestantism to the throne, while modernising the political system through peaceful means. Therefore, by the time that Queen Mary of Modena, went into labour, James had successfully managed to stir up dangerous anti-Catholic fears not seen since the Exclusion Crisis of 1679-81.

As per tradition of the time, Mary of Modena was not given privacy as she brought her baby into the world. The queen, her midwives and her ladies in waiting were all with her through her travail. Queen Mary's ten prior pregnancies had until now all resulted in miscarriages, stillbirths and death in infancy. So when a miraculously healthy male child was finally born, the leading Protestants started to panic. Within days James's enemies had used what should have been a joyous occasion and twisted it, causing rumours to be circulated about the newborn prince. The poor queen did not escape the callous gossip either. She was accused of never actually being pregnant but had dressed to make it look as if she was expecting a child. The rumours then claimed that Prince James Francis Edward was a changeling, smuggled into the birthing chamber within a copper a warming pan to make it look as if the queen had just given birth.

The subsequent political storm caused by these rumours surrounding the birth of the new prince got so bad that it forced his father to give a disposition to his Privy Council and to the Lords of the land. During this disposition the king had to name the seventy people who had been present as the queen gave birth. The disposition took place on 22 October 1688, but by this time it was too little too late.

Details of the disposition are recorded in the Calendar of State Papers:

> The Queen Dowager testified to having been present during the whole time of the Queen's Labour and delivery... the declarations of the king and the Queen Dowager, together with the disputations be in rolled in the court chancery.

> Calendar of State Papers, James II,
> Domestic series, June 1687 – February 1689, p.327)

Dispositions from forty witnesses, as well as all the medical staff who attended the royal birth, were recorded and enrolled in the court records. Regardless of what he could have done, James was never going to win over his enemies. Instead of settling these crises by addressing the rumours of legitimacy, by proving the young prince's legitimacy, James actually made things worse. Proving that his heir was legitimate merely served to convince his anti-Catholic opponents that they needed to depose him sooner rather than later to end the Catholic line of succession. The only way that James might have been able to calm the situation would have been to announce that his son would be raised in the Protestant faith. But this is something that James II would never have done.

From late summer 1688, leading Protestant men started to consider what they needed to do as a result of the birth of the new prince. During this time, leading Protestants had the opportunity to set up ideas on new political boundaries both within parliament and within the role of the monarch. These men considered their actions to be an act of faith to save the Protestant souls of the British nation. It could be argued that what was about to happen during the Glorious Revolution, was one of British history's most important events, politically, socially and religiously.

* * *

During the last years of Charles II's reign, a small number of English and Scottish Protestants had migrated to Europe as it was becoming apparent that the throne would pass to the Duke of York. They felt they had no choice but to do this despite the efforts of the Exclusionist cause and their attempts at changing the law, both through parliament and other less legal means. After Charles's death and the failed Monmouth Rebellion, more and more Protestants started to join those already in exile. Many settled in Flanders, the Dutch speaking area of Belgium, and within the Netherlands.

As his reign progressed, James failed to note the mood of the nations he ruled; instead of acting to reassure the Protestants he continued to antagonise them in an outdated and arrogant fashion as he pursued his own agenda. The solution was to find a way to replace James with a Protestant alternative and the most obvious choice was William of Orange. William was James's nephew via his sister Mary, and also his son-in-law because he had married James's daughter, also called Mary. The leading Protestants of 1688, needed to find a solution to achieve this without starting a protracted and bloody civil war. They also knew for any coup to work, they would need be plenty of funds and the operation had to be coordinated and planned from both the Netherland and Britain.

If we were to put an exact date on the start of the Glorious Revolution, then a good date to go with would be 30 June 1688. William of Orange had decided to accept an 'invitation' from seven English statesmen. These seven men would become known as the 'Immortal Seven'. These men were made up of the following prominent men of the age: the Earl of Shrewsbury, Charles Talbot; the Earl of Devonshire, William Cavendish; the Earl of Danby, Thomas Osborne; Viscount Richard Lumley, the Bishop of London; Henry Compton, 1st Earl of Orford; Edward Russell; and 1st Earl of Romney, Henry Sydney. These seven men came from a mixed political background and had joined forces in this time of political crisis. Political parties as we understand them in the twenty-first century were in their infancy in the late seventeenth century. MPs voted in parliament according to their consciences rather than in line with a particular political agenda or party line. The political two fractions were the Tories, who were traditionally Royalist and Anglican, and the Whigs which were more for political modernisation and were very anti-Catholic. Danby and the Bishop of London, Crompton, were both more aligned with the Tories while the other five men were more leaning towards Whig politics. In their invitation to the Prince of Orange they had invited him to invade England and Great Britain. They cited all of the ways in which James had endangered the religious and political state of Britain during his reign. So for the second time in his short reign, James faced an invasion from Europe. Both invasions were by nephews, one had hoped to displace him, the other wanted to defend the concerns of the nation.

William's acceptance of their invitation and their reasons for issuing it were not unexpected or new to the Stadholder. The Prince of Orange had been monitoring the political mood of Britain under his uncle's reign through the use of spies. William had his own personal and political agenda to invade Britain, but the invitation from the Immortal Seven was a much easier and neater way to achieve his goal. The reason William was happy to interfere in British politics was simple – he wanted to break up the British alliance with Louis XIV of France. The Netherlands and France had been embroiled in the Franco-Dutch wars, an ongoing series of wars over old tensions concerning Catholicism versus Protestantism in disputed territories, primarily made up of what we know as modern day Belgium. During the seventeenth century this area was known as Flanders and included areas such as Ghent and Ypres.

During the Civil Wars, the British alliance with France had offered refuge to Charles II and James when he was the Duke of York; their mother Henrietta Maria was French and Louis was their royal cousin. It was not until the Secret Treaty of Dover signed by Charles's Catholic ministers in 1670 that the alliance was more pronounced. As discussed earlier, Charles received an income in the form of a pension from his cousin, and in exchange Charles had to make sure that the Catholic James inherited his throne and that Britain supported the French in military campaigns. As a Protestant nation, Britain had traditionally supported fellow Protestant nations such as the Netherlands, rather than Catholic France; for the royal brothers, however, Louis's money gave them parliamentary freedom and was far more appealing – and cheaper – than fighting for the rights of fellow Protestant nations.

In the four months between receiving the invitation to 'investigate' James II and the Dutch force landing on British soil, William and Mary prepared and planned their strategy and learnt from previous mistakes. The Dutch needed to be prepared and equipped to deal with potential defence from James on two fronts. First, the small Dutch navy needed to be prepared if James deployed his far bigger and mightier Royal Navy. Second, they needed to be equipped and trained to deal with whatever land defences James may have set up. Ironically, James's army had benefited from the improvements implemented by Oliver Cromwell and his Parliamentarians during the Civil Wars of his father's reign.

William also had an additional domestic pressure which meant he needed to accomplish his aims in Britain swiftly, so that his Dutch territories were not left vulnerable to attack from Louis of France. The best way to achieve a quick resolution was to prepare as well as possible. The biggest affront to James's pride was that prior to the Immortal Seven writing to William, James had lent his nephew several British regiments. These men were still serving the Dutch at the time of the invasion and would have made other regiments feel brave enough to defect to William and his cause.

The Prince of Orange did not hide his intentions after receiving the formal invitation, and James's response to this threat did not start until late September. True to his weaker character it was too little too late and everything he tried was a desperate attempt to regain favour from those to whom he had behaved badly.

One of the first wrongs he tried to correct to make things easier for the Whig fraction in parliament. If he had thought about this properly he would have realised it would just make things easier for them to work with William and Mary rather than restore their loyalty.

James had also previously helped his fellow Catholics gain seats in parliament and positions at court, against the terms of the Test Acts. During September 1688, in a desperate act of compromise, he tried to reverse this and reinstate the law banning all Catholics from sitting in the next session of Parliament. This might have helped to pacify a few of his critics had he not then gone on and subsequently cancelled the next parliamentary session, thus making it an empty gesture.

An increasingly desperate James then tried to win back the Church of England and Anglican communion. At the beginning of his reign in 1685, James had gone after Henry Compton who, under the Restoration reign of Charles II, had held posts within the king's Privy Council, was the Dean of the Royal Chapel and oversaw the Protestant instruction of both Princess Mary and her sister Princess Anne. This continued even after their father James had converted to Rome. Problems between Compton and James came to ahead soon after James become king. The priest of the London parish of St Martins-in-the-field, John Sharp, preached a fiery anti-Catholic sermon to his parishioners and when he became aware of this, James instructed Compton to fire the priest from his living at St Martins. Compton refused to obey James and would go on to lose his places on the Privy Council and as the Dean of the Royal Chapel. At the end of 1688, James attempted to make amends to Compton by re-establishing the cleric to the Ecclesiastical commission. However this too would be another empty and rather insulting gesture, as James went on to scrap the commission two days after remitting Compton. Compton had a previous connection to one of his fellow Immortal Seven signatories before they wrote to William and Mary. In 1679, Thomas Osborne, then Lord Danby, had hired Compton to undertake a census examining the religious leanings and beliefs of Britain. This survey became known as the Compton Census.

Things were not looking good for the king and he was growing ever desperate and isolated. His next attempt to fix his reputation was to repair his relations with the academics in the Universities of Oxford and Cambridge. Earlier in his reign, James had decided to interfere in the administration of Oxbridge colleges. Initially removing Protestant facility with Catholic alternatives. Now he attempted to restore relations with these colleges by restoring the fellows he had removed. Evidence of this can be found in the Calendar of State Papers for James II in the following entry:

> October 13 1688: The King to the Master, President & Fellows of Gronville & cause college, Cambridge. Revoking his letter of 10 December [1686] and 21 July requiring them to admit Clement Boult MA, one of your fellows of the college ... and granting them full licence to elect into the same such persons as they shall think fit pursuant to the statutes of the college.
>
> (Calendar of State Papers James II, Domestic Series, June 1687 – February 1689. p.320)

Similar letters were sent to the college of St Mary Magdalen, Cambridge (ibid p.329) and Sidney Sussex college Cambridge too (ibid p.369).

This was not James's most desperate attempt to ward off invasion. The king actually tried to appease his nephew William and his daughter Mary by offering the compromise of staying neutral in any Dutch European squabbles. James was blinded by his desperation to the fact that his behaviour had already taken him beyond the point where such compromises would work; as well as the inability to see that William may have had his own motivations to invade.

By the time that his preparations were completed William had 20,000 soldiers, 5,000 horse for mounted Calvary and 500 vessels to carry both the men and supplies required for the task ahead. By comparison, James's defences were, on paper, bigger than the Dutch invaders. At his disposal he had a standing professional army of 25,000 men and about the same again of volunteer local militias.

William and his Protestant Armada landed in the Devonshire port of Torbay on a most auspicious day, 5 November – the anniversary of the foiling of the Gunpowder plot. If there was ever a good omen, this was surely it.

James's first error of judgement was to leave London twelve days after William had landed. The reason for leaving his capital vulnerable was that he had decided to go and meet his army who were congregated at Salisbury. By the time he had arrived, the king's mental state had deteriorated. The military man and hero of his youth did not reappear to help him at his moment of crisis. He also suffered from stress induced nose bleeds and insomnia. These nose bleeds are recorded in the following extract from the Calendar of State Papers:

Nov 21, Salisbury, The Earl of Middleton to Lord Preston: Yours of the 19th I received. His majesty ... was yesterday taken three or four times with bleeding at nose, and when he went to bed took diascordium.*

(Calendar of State Papers James II
domestic series junk 1687 – February 1689 pp.358)

James's despondent and reduced state made two of his most important and influential army leaders defect to William and Mary. The first was John Churchill, who had been helped to defeat the Monmouth Rebellion in 1685, three and half years previously. The other defector was the influential Duke of Grafton.

While the king was panicking in Salisbury, James's younger daughter Anne (later to be Queen Anne) had left London and headed towards territories in the Midlands that had already declared for William and his Protestant cause. 'The Cockpit: Princess Anne to William of Orange Nov 18: Conveying her best wishes and giving news that Prince George is to join him.' (Calendar of State Papers James II domestic series junk 1687 – Feb 1689 pp.357)

James arrived back in London mentally defeated on 23 November 1688. He was advised by the few councillors and courtiers that were still loyal to him to recall a parliament and issue his nephew William a royal pardon for his invasion. James ignored their advice; instead he opted to try and win Churchill back by sending the Earl of Godolphin to parley with Churchill and the Dutch. Williams response was to issue the following demands of his uncle the king; he needed to surrender the Tower of London and all the major Thames ports to William as well as proclaim to the people that he was in support of a free parliament. Naturally James did not comply with his nephew's demands. While Godolphin was negotiating for him, James had arranged for his wife, Mary of Modena, and their Catholic son to cross the channel in a safe French ship. The queen and Prince of Wales arrived in Calais on 21 December 1688, and this is recorded in

---

* Diascordium is an opiate used for pain relief and to aid sleep.

Sir David Nairne's papers. (*Sir David Nairne: The life of a Scottish Jacobite at the Court of Exiled Stuarts*, Corp, Edward, p.21) If James had had any sense, he would have joined his family and sailed with them to the safety of France – but of course he didn't.

On the evening of the 10 December 1688, King James II & VII found himself isolated and in fear. London had been infiltrated by Dutch forces. The last Catholic king of England and Britain had not been on his throne four years. He must have feared ending his reign and his life in the same manner as his father, Charles I – on a scaffold, under an executioners axe.

The Dutch invasion of the capital was led by Hendrik, Count Solms. The appearance of these men had, despite the late hour, caused a tension to run throughout the city of London. He marched the men up to the what was left of the Palace of Whitehall and demanded to be granted an audience with James. James, however had other ideas. Whether it was a knee jerk reaction made under intense fear or had been premeditated for this event of successful Dutch invasion, James decided to attempt to flee to Europe rather than face the Dutch. This decision is recorded in the state papers in a letter from the Earl of Feversham to William of Orange dated 11 December 1688:

> Having received this morning a letter from his majesty with the unfortunate news of his resolution to go out of England and that he s actually gone, I thought myself obliged, being at the head of his army … to let your highness know it, with the advice of all the officers here, as soon as it was possible to hinder the misfortune of effusion of blood.

> (Calendar of State Papers, Domestic,
> James II 1687–89, p.377)

Among the actions he took that fateful evening was the destruction of the legal writs drawn up to enable the calling of a new general election. He also took with him the great wax seal of his reign. The seal was the king's instrument permitted him to legally agree with political changes. While crossing the dark river Thames, James threw his royal seal into her murky waters. Both of these acts were done in the vain hope that this would disrupt the first days of the new regime in a constitutional way. In fact, James's actions proved exactly why he was losing his throne. Not only had he greatly misjudged and misunderstood the political landscape of his reign, but he had also failed to understand the political climate in a post-Restoration Britain. He was inflexible and rigid, failing to adapt to an evolving political society; writs and great seals were not necessary to make these great constitutional changes.

James's attempt for freedom was brought to an end by a group of fishermen from Kent. The Protestant men stopped him as they had mistaken the king for a fleeing Catholic priest; they frisked him, stole his money and desecrated a crucifix he was carrying. That particular crucifix held what James believed to have been a piece of the 'true cross'.

While James was attempting to escape, the people of London had sensed the change. The Protestant city saw the Dutch liberators as a welcome sign from God. Law and order disintegrated over the next forty-eight hours as this Protestant mob started to target and attack prominent Catholics homes and desecrate Catholic churches and chapels, looting them for all their wealth. The mob also targeted the notorious Judge Jeffreys, who had ruled harshly over the participants of the failed Monmouth Rebellion. Jefferys was saved minutes before the mob were going to lynch him. Instead he was taken to the Tower of London for his own 'safety'. He never left and died of kidney failure in April the following year.

The standing army had moved from Salisbury and were at this point based in the west London town of Uxbridge. If these men were left to their own devices, with access to weapons the situation outside of London may have disintegrated into violent mob activity. Thankfully a significant number of these well trained men decided to seek out and join the Dutch invasion force rather than participate in mob behaviour.

The Army under James, had been made up of men from all parts of his territory, including men from Catholic Ireland. The Republic of Ireland is still primarily Catholic today; in Northern Ireland, today as in the seventeenth century, the population is split between Protestant and Catholic. The religious tensions in Northern Ireland have influenced politics in the region right into the twenty-first century. The Irishmen recruited from northern areas of the country, who had only days ago been seen as comrades, now found themselves vulnerable; fighting on opposing sides to, and fearing, their former pals. General fear of the Catholic Irish population in England was far greater outside of the capital and was being fuelled by false rumours in cities such as Birmingham. The rumours insinuated that James was organising a counter-invasion using the Catholic Irish to face the Dutch Protestants. This was unhelpful to the Irish soldiers stranded in London.

On the night of the 12 December 1688, the Irish population of the city prepared themselves for potential attack from their Protestant neighbours. Thankfully a massacre did not happen. Many of the Irish travelled to northern ports such as Liverpool in the hopes of getting a boat back home. Most of the Irish soldiers returned their weapons to the artillery based in the Tower of London, and in an exchange they were given the wages they were owed. Although there were no mass killings, these events show that the 'Glorious Revolution' was not as smooth or as peaceful as its name implies.

Although some Dutch troops had entered London, William had not joined instead waiting for an invitation from the officials of London inviting William to the city. This arrived from the Major of London on 17 December and is recorded in the state papers:

> Humble thanks to your highness for your progress in your great and glorious undertaking for preserving our religion, laws and liberties ... humbly desire your

highness to accept the tender of our readiness to prepare or appoint a convenient place for your reception within this city'.

(Calendar of State Papers Domestic series
June 1686 – February 1688 pp.381)

The crowds came out to welcome and cheer but before William was within the boundaries of the capital he received news that James had been caught and returned to London. William needed to be careful how he proceeded in order to avoid mass hysteria and London turning violent. Sensibly he halted his victorious entrance into the capital, and issued his uncle with the following demand: leave London in the next ten hours.

The chances of his uncle James complying with his demand were high. He had been attempting to flee and had thrown away his great seal prior to being caught. William wanted to make sure his uncle did not cause any disruptions as he left so he sent Dutch armed men to escort the fallen king out of the city. It was on this journey that James was able to sneak away from his escort. We will never know if he was supposed to escape or not, but having James escape to France and unharmed, was rather a tidy solution for William. James took a small boat across the channel to join his family. James II once again found himself in exile and seeking help from his cousin Louis XIV.

In a matter of weeks William had successfully invaded Britain and dethroned his uncle in a relatively peaceful manner and the populace at large were supportive. Politically there were more complex issues and decisions to be resolved and made going forward, but the Protestant majority collectively sighed with relief that James was gone.

The big question was how did the politicians within their various factions want to move forward politically and constitutionally? There was not one idea that was preferred, they seemed to be open to all possible solutions across the board, regardless of political alliance.

Some favoured William, seeing him as the second conqueror. Others preferred the idea of Mary being sovereign as she was James's daughter from his first marriage. This would technically mean that succession had not been broken and it was through a Protestant line of the Stuarts. Then there was the idea of a joint reign, with both William and Mary ruling as equals and working with rather than controlling a parliament. The only thing that mattered was resolving this quickly to avoid a constitutional crisis.

The first of the possible options to be ruled out was Mary ruling as queen, and while William was consort to his wife, the Prince of Orange was determined to be central to the construction of this new constitution and political system. William was proactive and set up an interim governing body as a stop-gap government. This executive body was made up of powerful men who had previously served Charles II in his Privy Council and last parliament. This was a very deliberate move on William's part, he wanted to make it clear from day one, that he did not approve of his father-in-law's way of governing and aligned himself with Anglican Protestants rather than Catholics.

As early as the 21 December 1688, William was asked to become king by his new executive body. But true to William's nature, he did not accept straight away as he wanted to ensure that he agreed with whatever role he would play within this new constitution. The executive body William had first put together would become known as the Convention of 1689 and on 22 January 1689, he started a process to establish how England and Ireland should be ruled. (Scotland would get a separate convention in March 1689). After seven days of debate, argument and compromises, the convention decided and ruled that the only option that would prevent a future constitutional crises was to bar Catholics from inheriting the throne. Britain therefore needed a new Protestant monarch.

The Convention of 1689, ruled on the 6 February that William and his wife Mary were to rule jointly. This was the best compromise as Mary fulfilled the criteria of directly inheriting the throne from her father, while William was also suitably related to James as his nephew and son-in-law. Mary had not wanted to rule as queen in her own right so this was the best compromise.

By 12 February, the convention had compiled what has become known as the Declaration of Right. This legal statement establishes in law and on paper what has been agreed upon as the wrongs of James II while he was monarch. They found that he had broken the law and harmed the nation thirteen ways during his short reign. The main points are as follows:

James passed laws without using the parliamentary process, he prosecuted individuals who had critiqued him or his reign, he actively disregarded laws previously made to fulfil his own agenda, including promoting and employing openly practicing Roman Catholics in positions within court or the civil or military services. This is going directly against the Test Acts of 1673 and 1678. He maintained a large standing army during peacetime without justification or parliamentary approval. He misused monies that had been granted to the crown, by parliament, for other purposes. He disarmed Protestants while allowing Catholics to carry weapons. He carried out roles usually conducted by parliament when he wanted to manipulate the outcome in his favour. He was also criticised for issuing high bail charges or fines as well as imposing cruel and illegal punishments including confiscating property from people prior to being tried or convicted. He did this against people he personally did not like and regardless of their alleged or proven crimes.

These findings are rather damning, showing James to be a greedy and vindictive man and are indicative of the mean, jealous and insecure streak in his personality. These traits had been evident since childhood and again when he was an adolescent and younger man during his brother's reign – both while in exile and then when the Crown was restored. These traits just became more exaggerated after he became king. He justified his behaviour to himself as he believed, like his doomed father did, in the idea of the Divine Rights of Kings.

Despite the fate of his father, James became over confident as he had witnessed the later part of his brother reign.

The Convention used James's errors as the base of their new constitution in order to make sure that the same mistakes could not be to be made again by William and Mary, and all subsequent monarchs after them.

Prior to their coronation on the 11 April 1689, William and Mary needed to agree to the new constitution and this new form of monarchy. The new limitations effectively made the future monarchs head of state, therefore handing over the law-making and justices of the nation to the 'elected' House of Commons and the hereditary peers that make up the House of Lords. Furthermore, they separated the head of the Anglican church, the monarch, from parliament to stop the reoccurring issue of faith interfering in politics; a problem that had dogged the reigns of all the monarchs since the death of Henry VIII in 1547. These new legal limitations forbade, in law, anyone inheriting the throne who is a practising Roman Catholic, as well as prohibiting them from actively promoting the Catholic faith within their realm. Freedom of speech in parliament was to be reinstated, even if it was critical of the monarch. The monarch was also required to be independent of the justice system. They would no longer be able to place corrupt or biased jurors or judges in any legal situation. Most importantly, the monarch would be acting as a head of state. This meant that it was imperative that the parliamentary, governing body needed to be held frequently.

Of course this is a long way from the democracy and universal suffrage that we understand and have today in Great Britain. However, it was the foundation that allowed us to get to this point today. It also created a fair and unbiased justice system that gave everyone the right to trial and be innocent until proven guilty. The separation of the church from the state, also helped create the multi-faith society of modern Britain. This is why the events of the Glorious Revolution and the fall of James II are an important and critical milestone in British social political and constitutional history.

Ireland and the Williamite War
1689–1691

The departure of James II & VII from his kingdoms and the desertions of his responsibilities as monarch are best described by Dalrymple in his memoirs when he said the following of James's flight:

> Calm and relief from anxiety, not pity for him, not indignation against him; the weakness of his behaviour having stifled those passions equally in the breast of his friends and of his foes.

(Dalrymple; *Memoirs of Great Britain and Ireland 1790* p.187)

James's behaviour during the last weeks of his reign was noticeably out of character. It is worth looking into what may have caused these changes. As noted in the previous chapter, James was, on paper, in the stronger position militarily compared to William's smaller invading force. If James had presented himself as a proactive, strong military leader and commander when he visited Churchill and Grafton, his strongest military generals might not have defected to William. Their desertion effectively weakening James's military advantage. Having grown up through the Civil Wars and, following the execution of his father, spending most of his formative years in exile fighting in wars around Europe, as well as serving as a Naval Admiral during the Anglo-Dutch wars of his brother's reign – James's response to Williams invasion in 1688 are very out of character.

One possible answer to the king's out of character behaviour could be that he had suffered a mental health crisis. What we do know is that, understandably, he suffered with stress and had nose bleeds as a result. His brother, Charles II, was also known to suffer from nose bleeds when under extreme pressure – most famously, after the Battle of Worcester, in 1651. James also suffered from insomnia during the end of 1688 and displayed indecisive behaviour, which was extremely out of character and both symptoms of general stress and anxiety.

Another possibility could be that he could have had a minor stroke during this time. In 1688, James would have been 55 years old, and although strokes can happen at any age, to anyone, James did have a family history of them. Charles is thought to have had a minor stroke in August 1679, prior to the large stroke that eventually took his life in February 1685. James himself would suffer a stroke just prior to his death in 1701, so it is a possibility. Even after a mini stroke, there can be changes to the temperament and behaviour of recovering patients.

Of course, this is conjecture informed by educated guesses based on the information available. There is no sure way of knowing what caused James to act so differently in 1688, but it is worth exploring in order to understand why he acted as he did at this important time because it did ultimately contribute to the loss of his throne.

Whatever the cause of the changes to James's behaviour, he did flee to France and settled into a new life. He was welcomed and treated with kindness and support from his royal cousin, Louis XIV. Louis, who was not known for his sensitivity, ensured that James was treated with the respect and dignity of a monarch by those within his court. As a result, James soon regained his sense of poise and the grandeur of being an anointed king as well as some of his old fighting spirit.

As early as February 1689, French ships were being prepared off the Brittany coastline to in order to carry James and some French support to Ireland – James's only former Catholic country. The plan was to re-establish James as king in Ireland, then to gather and train an Irish army so he could fight William and his daughter Mary in order to retake the thrones of England and Scotland.

The French invasion fleet consisted of thirteen French warships and nine smaller vessels. Louis also equipped James with enough weaponry and arms to train and equip and Irish army of 20,000 men. In addition to this he also supplied 4,500 French armed men to help him with his plan to try and re-establish a Jacobite government in Ireland.

Dalrymple gives an account of James's arrival in Ireland in the *Siege of Derry*:

> James found the appearance of thing in Ireland equal to his wishes ... his old army steady, and a new one raised ... the Protestants over the greater part of Ireland disarmed; the province of Ulster alone in disobedience ... no English troops in the kingdom no fleet on the coast, his reception at Kinsale and Cork cordial and his public entry into Dublin magnificent.

> (*Siege and History of Londonderry*
> Dalrymple in Hempton pp.15–16)

Unlike Scotland and England, the island of Ireland had always been the most sympathetic and favourable towards James. Unlike both England and Scotland, Ireland's Reformation did not result in a national change in Christian denomination and Roman Catholicism had remained dominant. During the interregnum under Oliver Cromwell, specifically between 1649 and 1653, the Cromwellian war in Ireland had taken place. English persecution of the Irish would take on a new and crueller persecution of the Catholic majority. Memories were long and the people of Ireland did not forget their treatment at Protestant hands. With the return of the monarchy during the Restoration, the Catholics could one again return and participate in the Irish parliament. Charles half-heartedly attempted to make amends for the damage caused by Cromwell, but only one third of the land confiscated by Cromwell and the New Model Army was ever returned to the original Irish Catholic owners. This half-hearted

117

attempt and reparation was overseen by Richard Talbot, later Earl of Tyrconnell. The impact of Cromwell and the inadequate reparations by Charles II meant that resentment bubbled under the surface of the Irish nation towards their Protestant English overlords. So when James fled to France in late 1688, the Irish Catholics were the obvious choice for James to seek support from against William.

James was an old comrade of Richard Talbot, who he later created the Earl of Tyrconnell. James and Talbot had met while James was still the Duke of York and in exile before the death of Oliver Cromwell. After Charles regained the throne in 1660, Talbot became Charles's man on the spot in Ireland and oversaw the half-hearted attempt at re-appropriation of land to Catholics. The pair's association was greatly strengthened after James accessed to the throne in 1685. Upon the creation and bestowing of the title Earl of Tyrconnell to Talbot, James granted him the position of Viceroy of Ireland. In return Tyconnell carried out a pro-Catholic agenda in all areas of civil and military administration, replacing the Protestants civil servants with loyal Irish Catholics. By the time of the Glorious Revolution, Ireland was a Catholic stronghold.

After James escaped to France, the Earl of Tyrconnell had started to recruit, train and build up the Irish army. The recruitment drive was extremely successful and he managed to draft an additional 9,000 soldiers and 3,000 mounted cavalry men to for his pro-Catholic driven cause. By the time the French party was ready to bring James to Ireland, Tyrconnell had a Catholic force of 45,000 ready to fight.

As early as November 1688 Protestants and non-conformist preachers and ministers reached out to William of Orange as they could foresee the violent vengeance the Irish Catholics wanted to inflict on their Protestant neighbours. A delegation from the northern Irish province of Ulster met William on 26 December 1688, to express their fears and request his help. Five days prior to this delegation, exiled Irish Protestants also sought an audience with William to express their fears of what they felt was a dangerous situation developing in Ireland. In January 1689, Scottish Presbyterians, who were deeply concerned for fellow Scottish Protestants based in the north of Ireland also communicated their concerns to William. The following month, the Scots sent arms and ammunition to their comrades in Derry so their fellow Presbyterians had them to use in defence against any Irish Catholic violence.

William had been made very aware of the Protestant cause on Irish soil from the beginning of his British campaign. He reiterated these concerns to his Conventional Parliament when they met in January 1689, but he knew, in order for him to successfully help the Protestant plight in Ireland, he needed to be in a firmer position upon the British mainland.

Even before William and James met on the shores of Ireland, the nation had started to divide along lines of Christian denomination. Cities such as Enniskillen and Derry were among the first to stop cooperating with Tyrconnell. The Protestants, who were mainly situated in the north, started to form an opposing armed wing to match the Catholic forces fronted by Tyrconnell. Unlike many counter-Reformation struggles on the European mainland, the divisions on the island of Ireland were not divided cleanly with Catholics for James and Protestants for William. Localities and other agendas were considered before factions took sides in the impending war.

Although Tyrconnell was Catholic and loyal to James, he had his own motivations for taking his position in the war. He did not represent all Irish Catholics and rather than seeing James back upon the British and Irish thrones, his motives were to help the small minority of landed Irish Catholics who had regained their land under Charles II.

Other people and areas of note include Arthur Rawdon, who rallied large numbers of Protestant men to join William's cause in the north. Although primarily Protestant, Derry started out as pro-James and anti-Tyrconnell. Belfast on the other hand was very pro-William from the start.

For the purpose of this book, the Williamite war in Ireland from 1689–91 will primarily focus on the British domestic aspects of the conflict between William and James. However, there were other consequences with wider implications, primarily dealing with the ongoing tensions between the Dutch Republic and France. James II's crisis and the invite from the Immortal Seven was an opportunity too good not to manipulate. It opened up the chance for William to gain access to an additional strong military force, in his attempt to defeat Louis XIV.

On 8 March 1689, the English parliament had passed a motion agreeing to supply William with 22,000 trained men, made up of both British and European mercenaries, to help him deal with James's impending invasion of Ireland. The French invasion party with James arrived at the southern Irish port of Kinsale in County Cork on 12 March 1689, four days after William had been granted extra support from the English Parliament.

The gambit of the Wlliamite war took place during April 1689, when James II attempted to take command of the city of Derry for the second time. The subsequent events that unfolded would show the true nature and spirit of the city of Derry, as well as the bravery of her people who faced attack, starvation and disease because they stood up for their beliefs.

To fully understand the strong feelings of the City of Derry and why its citizens acted as they did, it is important to look at events in Ireland as the Glorious Revolution unfolded in England. In a small Ulster hamlet called Comber, a letter was discovered that would have a catastrophic consequences. What became known as the 'Comber letter' was discovered in December 1688; the contents are said to have had detailed plans stating that the local Irish Catholics were going to carry out a massacre, killing Protestants and sparing no one regardless of age or gender. If this had happened, it would have been an Irish event on the scale of the St Bartholomew Day massacre of 1572, when thousands of Protestants were killed in Paris and other areas of France. Although it didn't happen, the discovery of the letter would still cause a great many innocent deaths.

One of those consequences was that fear and suspicion were now running high among the local population. Tyrconnell thought that sending for a regiment of Scots might help ease tensions within the region. Ulster, and particularly the city of Derry, had high percentage of Presbyterian Protestants who had migrated from Scotland. A regiment known as the Redshanks were commanded to come over to the province of Derry. Although the Redshanks were Scottish, they were not going to sooth the troubled waters as they were very loyal to James II. Given Tyrconnell's background, one would have expected him to have foreseen this potential problem.

When the people of Derry saw the army of Redshanks approaching, local dignitaries met to decide if they should grant them entry into the city. The Anglican Bishop of the city, Ezekiel Hopkins, wanted to welcome the guards, his argument being that James II was still the crowned monarch and it was the right thing to do, even if James was Catholic. The Presbyterian faction led by James Gordon disagreed. They wanted to lock the Redshanks out of the city because they feared that the guards may carry out the plans discovered in the Comber letter.

While the dignitaries argued, thirteen of the city's apprentices decided to take the matters out of the lawmakers hands and took action. They ran to the city gate, known as Ferry Key, and locked the gates and doors fast. When news of this reached Dublin, Tyrconnell was not well pleased.

Derry's rebellious spirit spread through Ulster and similar actions were taken in Enniskillen, who also decided to bar Tyrconnell's men out of their city. All these events were happening as William secured England and James fled to the safety of France. The settled Protestants of Ireland found themselves on high alert, fearing what may happen both at home and over the Irish sea in England.

William's position in England became more secure. The Glorious Revolution had effectively achieved its goal and the year changed to 1689. The fears of the people of Ireland were once again stirred up when the deposed James II landed upon their shores with French troops. They knew that his presence would divide their nation. While he used their home as a command post from which to launch a campaign, to try and reclaim first Ireland and then Scotland and England. It did not take long for Derry to declare their support – not for James, but for the new monarchy of William and Mary. They knew they would be one of James's first targets. If he could get this previously disobedient Protestant city to obey him, then other towns and cities would follow. Also, given Ulster's links to Scotland, if James secured a major base for immigrant Scottish Protestants, it was thought that this may help to smooth James's path to regaining the Scottish throne.

The Jacobites' over confidence had been boosted two days after James arrived, when a skirmish took place near Dromore in County Down. It had been an easy victory for them and gave them a false perception of what they might face in the coming days and weeks. In the aftermath of their small victory, they decided not to pursue their defeated opponents, which in turn allowed the losing side to get word to Derry. This was a crucial strategic error made early on in the campaign. The element of surprise was lost.

On 14 April 1689, the Jacobites crossed the River Foyle by the town of Strabane about fifteen miles from Derry. Four days later, James II rode up to the Bishop's Gate entrance of the city and demanded to be admitted. While he was pompously making his demand he also enlightened the city about what he expected of them when they meekly surrendered. Derry responded by firing at the dethroned king from the city's defensive walls.

The men in the in the defensive ramparts fired at James because he was unaware of an agreement that had been struck between the dignitaries of the city and one of his Jacobites, John Hamilton. In this agreement, Hamilton had promised the city of Derry that no Jacobite army would approach the city. And here was James, at the head of his army, demanding to be let in. It is little wonder that the guards fired and felt they could not trust his words. Despite the Redshanks being locked out in December, James had expected the city's gates to be open and for Derry obey him. The cause of this misjudgement was that four days earlier, the city's governor, Robert Lundy, had helped James and his Jacobites cross the River Foyle. Consequently, Lundy was very uncomfortable with the city firing on James; he would have preferred to surrender to the man whom he still considered his king. Lundy was in a minority. Adam Murray, a young Ulster Scotsman and solider stood up to Lundy and urged him to fight for Derry's freedom and her people. Realising he was in a minority and unwilling to change his view, Lundy relinquished his governorship of the city. Murray had won the argument. His message to the anxious people of the city was clear and simple: 'No Surrender'.

Although the city had been closed off since December 1688, it was now that the real siege of Derry began. With Lundy in disgrace, Murray was invited to take over as the governor of the city, though he politely declined the offer; although he had the natural ability and qualities of a good leader, he preferred to remain a serving solider. The governorship was jointly appointed to Henry Baker and George Walker and they wasted no time in their new post.

Battle and defence plans were drawn up and agreed upon, food and arms stores were inspected and itemised. Daily rations were announced and implemented; 7,340 soldiers and officers were rallied and rounded up from within Derry and 10,000 of the city's inhabitants decided to take their leave before the bombardment started. The Jacobites were happy to let these people flee to safety, mainly because they hoped to glean some useful information and intelligence from them. Once again the Jacobites underestimated the people of Derry: none of those who fled obliged. The evacuation of those 10,000 people did, however, help those left behind, as this would allow the limited stores of food and fresh water to stretch further with less mouths to feed. The number of brave souls who chose to remain within the confines of the city walls has been estimated at 20,000.

As his plans had not gone as smoothly as he had expected, true to character James decided to retreat from the battle lines to the safety of Dublin, leaving his French general, de Maumout, and Hamilton in charge of the Jacobites. On 21 April, the bombardment of the city walls started. This was not very effective as the Jacobites were not armed with the correct weaponry to make any impact on the strong defensive walls. The only damage they managed to cause was when a number of smaller cannonballs made it over the walls unhindered, damaging buildings near the city boundaries.

Adam Murray was busy outside the city barricades fighting the Jacobites strategically and effectively. One mile north of the city walls was a small village called Pennyburn. While defending the village, Murray and his comrades were able to take out two French Jacobite leaders, de Maumout and de Pusignan as well as keeping the village in Williamite control.

After the village was secure in Williamite hands, Murray and his men moved on to defend the next important site, Windmill Hill. The hill was located closer to the city's walls near the Bishop's Gate entrance. In this fight Murray and his soldiers killed around 200 Jacobites and once again kept hold of this important strategic point.

By the end of May 1689, 3,000 Jacobites had been killed in the siege – a siege they had started. Skirmishes and attacks against the strong walls of Derry continued. Hunger, sickness and poor morale were affected both sides of the barricade. But still the attacks and bombardments continued on all of the exterior walls.

Seven weeks into the siege, on the 3 June 1689, the Jacobites started to throw bombs into the city over the walls. This, not unsurprisingly, caused the tired, sick and hungry of the city to panic. When these bombs hit a surface with force, not only did they explode, they would shatter, causing the pieces of shrapnel to fly at force. Injuries sustained from the shrapnel caused nasty wounds and nearly always resulted in death.

It was around this time that the people of Derry had a moment of hope when they saw three small ships from England sailing up the River Foyle. These three boats had come across the Irish sea and almost made it to their final destination, but the Jacobites had found a way to stop much needed relief arriving to the desperate people of Derry. In the weeks prior to the arrival of these ships, the Jacobites had decided to prepare for such an eventuality by erecting a boom across the Foyle. This barricade over the water was made up of a floating log bridge, held together by cables that stretched across the girth of the river. At each end of the floating structure were gunners ready to fire at stationary boats on their way towards Derry. It was a seventeenth-century version of a police stinger, but for boats.

Even though the aid was stopped from reaching the city, the Jacobites decided their best course of action was to attempt to take Windmill Hill again. This was a poor strategy as the Williamite kept control of the hill, while the Jacobites lost more men in their failed attempt. What's more, it did not stop the help trying to get to Derry.

On the 13 June, more ships from England were spotted approaching the boom, en route to Derry. The new ships joined the original three, yet none of the aid vessels attempted to find a way to get their desperately needed supplies, to the people of Derry. While this was frustrating to the Williamites and defenders of Derry, the sight of the ships, was a morale booster to the Jacobites; the boom had done its job.

Hungry and desperate people do desperate things and on 18 June, a desperate mob stormed Governor Walker's quarters because they suspected that he was hording food. Walker and Baker both knew it was vital to try to get a message to the English ships. It seems the relief flotilla were just as eager to get a message to Derry. The captain of the main vessel, Kirke, used a member of his crew known as Roache to take a message to the city. Roache was able to get through unnoticed and swim up the River Foyle.

Upon receiving the message, George Walker replied to Kirke, relaying the conditions and urgent need for aid. Upon his return Roache was less lucky; he was spotted by the Jacobites who shot the messenger. Although wounded, Roache managed to get back to the city. A second messenger was found, and again an attempt was made to reply to Kirke. The unknown messenger tried to swim in the dark to avoid detection but drowned in his attempt. His body was washed up and found early the next day by the Jacobites. They took his corpse and strung it up within sight of the city walls; the Jacobites' message to the defenders of Derry was clear – your message was not delivered and we know how bad things are within the walls. The Jacobites now knew that their plan to starve the city was working.

The next calamity to strike the city happened when one of the joint governors, Henry Baker, fell ill and died. Frustration caused the Jacobites to attempt to resolve the situation by diplomatic means again. In the talks the Jacobites offered safe passage to those who wanted to leave the desperate conditions of the city and promised that those who remained would be protected. Derry refused and decided to keep holding firm in their policy of No Surender, even though the people within the city walls were now living off the flesh of dead horses and domestic animals such as cats and dogs, as well as resorting to vermin including rats and mice. This is recorded in Dalrymple's account of the siege:

> the weather grew sultry, disease at last seized them cooped up in a narrow place. They buried 15 officers in one day. Baker their governor died … their provisions being spent, they preserved life by eating horse flesh, tallow starch salted hides, impure animals and roots vegetables'

(Siege and History of Londonderry
Dalrymple in Hempton, pp.15–16)

Governor Walker noted in his diary the prices of food in the city's market during the hardest point in the siege:

Horse flesh sold for 1s 8d
  per pound
A dogs head 2s 6d
A rat 1s 0d
A pound of tallow 4s 0d
A pound of salted hides 1s 0d

A quarter dog 5s 6d
A cat 4s 6s
A mouse 0s 6d
A horse pudding 0s 6d
A quart of horse blood 1s 0d

(Siege and History of Londonderry,
Walker in Hempton, p.132)

Frustrated with the lack of progress, James arranged for a change of leadership for his men at Derry. The man he sent was Conrad de Rosen, who arrived on 20 June. Conrad de Rosen, also known just as von Rosen, was born in modern-day Latvia. He had a military career within the Swedish army before being expelled in disgrace. In an attempt to establish his military career, he joined the French army. Here he thrived and in 1646 had been given his own regiment. He was part of the invading party who arrived in Ireland with James II on 12 March. Von Rosen's tactics were nothing like those of Hamilton – he was a tough man of war and didn't mind how he achieved his goal. Von Rosen ordered local Protestants in Ulster to be rounded up, stripped naked and marched to the main gates of Derry. This emotional blackmail was intended to bring things to a swift end, but von Rosen greatly underestimated both his captors and the defenders of the city. As the naked Protestants were congregated outside Derry in a state of humiliation, von Rosen gave the city an ultimatum: let your fellow Protestants in or watch them die. The naked prisoners shouted to the people of Derry not to let them in and to hold firm in a selfless and brave act of solidarity.

Derry's response to the Jacobites was just as hostile: if you kill these innocent people, we will hang our Jacobite prisoners over the city walls. Von Rosen could see no way out of this and so let the local Protestants go. Meanwhile, John Hamilton had written to James describing the behaviour of Von Rosen. James, to his credit, was angered by the reports of von Rosen's behaviour and ordered him to return to France. Derry had out-foxed the Jacobites again, despite their desperate conditions and it was much needed morale boost.

Hunger was not the problem facing the defenders of Derry. By this stage in the siege, the city's sanitation and public hygiene was causing disease. Corpses of animals and humans were decaying without being dealt with, water was in limited supply and the street ran with raw excrement and sewage – both animal and human. The smell must have been atrocious. Between disease and starvation the defenders were down to 5,000 fighting men behind the city walls. As conditions worsened, the number of deaths increased daily. And yet frustratingly, the fleet of English ships was still at anchor in view of the city.

On Sunday 13 July, the two sides called a temporary truce so that they could parley upon on the contested Windmill Hill. This momentary ceasefire would be one of the pivotal moments of the siege, giving the Williamites of Derry hope that they might still be able to win this epic battle of wills. As the representatives of the city started negotiations, one half of the governors of the city, George Walker, remained within the walls to take stock of the stores. While he was working in his office, an adolescent boy entered and handed him a missive. The note was from Captain Kirke of the English fleet. The ships had weighed anchor and relocated to the nearby Island of Inch, in County Donegal. Here they were awaiting additional back up from England.

Governor Walker's reply did not sugar-coat the conditions within the city walls; he told Kirke that the aid needed to get to the city by the 26 July or they would be forced to surrender to the Jacobites' demands. The messenger boy bravely started to take the missive back to the English ships at Inch Island. It was a clever tactic to use a young lad to carry the message. In most cases a boy out and about would not attract the attentions of the Jacobites, they would assume he was out playing or a local urchin. To give the people of the city renewed hope Walker cropped the letter, changing it to imply that Kirke already had the English back up and rescue was near.

The negotiations on Windmill Hill had come to stalemate. The representatives from the city knew they had until 26 July, while the Jacobites were eager to bring the siege to an end much sooner. The two sides retreated for the night and decided to retry the following day. When the negotiators reported back to Walker, he confided that the morale-boosting letter was doctored, forcing them all to concede that they would need to negotiate a surrender. When it came to agreeing to terms the next day, the two sides could not agree, and the talks ended, breaking the brief ceasefire. A lot now relied on that messenger boy and the English relief ships.

Four days later on 19 July, Kirke's messenger returned. The new note promised that the fleet would act as soon as they could. Once again Walker took a risk, but by this point he and the defenders of the city had nothing to lose. In his reply, he told Kirke that the boom and its accompanying gun stations had been removed from the River Foyle – this was not true but Walker knew he had to force the relief fleet to act and this was the option he had in the current situation.

The wheels had been set in motion; things would have to come to a conclusion soon, one way or another. On his way back to Donegal, the lad was stopped by a group of sharp-eyed Jacobites; he was questioned and held for two days, but the courageous youth did not tell the enemy anything. He arrived back at the fleet with his missive unread by the Jacobites. Upon reading Walker's reply, Kirke started to prepare to go back to the River Foyle; Walker's risk had done its job. The English ships left Inch island and moored at the mouth of the River Foyle. They rested at Culmore Point so that they could use favourable tides and winds to help them in their mission. By this point the siege had entered the 100th day and things were desperate. The defenders had lost 600 more fighting men to starvation and disease. On Sunday 31 July, Walker – who was also a preacher – told his congregation that he had hope that God would relieve them very soon. God must have heard Derry's prayers that day as the tides and winds changed and the English ships set sail up the River Foyle for the second time.

The leading ship of the fleet was called the *Mountjoy* and of course they soon discovered that Walker had lied to them and the Jacobites started firing. The ships were sitting ducks and a battle with the *Mountjoy* began. As shots were exchanged from both sides of the riverbank, a boat of men rowed up to the boom and cut the cords holding the logs together. When the cords snapped with help from the strong tides, the *Mountjoy* and the rest of the English aid vessels sailed through the ruins of the boom. The Jacobites knew that they had lost this grudge match and that Derry would soon have fresh help and supplies. Over the next few days, the Jacobites started to retreat, leaving the site of the siege and the surrounding areas; Derry had held out and won.

It is not known how many of the 20,000 civilians that chose to remain in Derry died during the 105 days they were locked in. The estimates range from the conservative 4,000 to a staggering 10,000 – half the population – that would have been made up of men women and children. The figure for military deaths was recorded by Governor Walker and he lost just under 2,000 men, mostly to starvation and disease rather than fighting.

The following was recorded in Governor Walker's diary of the siege giving dates and numbers of the garrison of men within Derry's wall:

> July 8 the garrison now is reduced to 5,520 men
> July 13 the garrison now is reduced to 5,313 men
> July 17 the garrison now is reduced to 5,114 men
> July 22 the garrison now is reduced to 4,973 men
> July 25 the garrison now is reduced to 4,892 men

> (*Siege and History of Londonderry*
> Walker in Hempton, p.131)

All in all, Derry had paid an extremely heavy price for William of Orange, his cause, Protestantism and the city's freedom. Although the later Battle of the Boyne is better remembered than the Siege of Derry, I would argue that the events over those 105 day were far more important to the Protestant cause and the eventual victory of the Williamite war in Ireland.

According to Governor Walker, the Jacobites 'lost between eight or nine thousand men before our walls and a hundred of their best officers' (*Siege and History of Londonderry*, Walker in Hempton, p.134). It is worth remembering that Walker is writing his notes from the perspective of the victorious side and he had only intelligence and hearsay from captured prisoners to make these assessments. Although conditions were by no means great outside of the walls, they were significantly better than the conditions within the besieged city and should be taken with a grain of salt.

On 4 August, 2,000 Jacobites were set upon and killed by Williamites near a place called Newtownbutler, in county Fermanagh. A further 500 Jacobites tried to escape in the nearby Lough Erne and many perished by drowning in the deep waters. Despite these defeats at the hands of William's men, the Jacobites and James continued to try to subdue the people of Ireland, and one of the ways James tried to achieve this was by setting up the Patriot Parliament. As James was establishing himself in Ireland, William remained in London, settling into his new role as king as well as keeping abreast of his interests on mainland Europe. James's presence in Ireland was just another front for him to tackle in his ongoing war with France. It wasn't until fifteen months after James had arrived in Ireland that William set about facing him.

On 14 June 1690, William and his army arrived at the Irish port of Carrickfergus Bay, that is known today as Belfast Lough. William's invasion party was made up of 1,100 ships and 36,000 men of a variety of nationalities, as well as English soldiers. The percentages were approximately as follows: 7,000 Danes, 6,000 Dutch, 3,000 Huguenot French Protestants, 14,000 men in British uniform. There were an additional 6,000 men from Ireland who joined up with William's men, many of whom had taken part in sieges at Enniskillen and Derry and were unhappy with James and his Jacobites. The new English king disembarked his flotilla at 15.00 on the day of his arrival. From there the invasion party progressed into Belfast. William was warmly welcomed by the locals who rejoiced and celebrated with bonfires and parties. In Belfast, William met with his commanders to start planning how to deal with James – for William felt it was imperative that the war on the Irish front should be concluded swiftly so he could refocus on Louis XIV. It was decided that William and his army needed to relocate to Dublin in order to secure the city for their side.

While traveling towards the capital, William received intelligence that his party were likely to meet James's Jacobite army before they reached Dublin. This is exactly what happened and it turned out to be one of the most important moments in both British and Irish history, as well as James II's life.

* * *

On the last day of June 1690 the two rival armies caught sight of each other over the River Boyne. William and his larger army were on the north bank while James and his smaller force were situated on the southern bank. Unlike the Williamite force, the rag-tag army of the Jacobites were predominantly made up of local men with little to no previous military experience. These were the men that James had recruited and partly trained in the previous fifteen months before this battle. In addition to these local men, James also had a small regiment of experience French soldiers supplied by Louis XIV.

Both camps spent the rest of the day in councils of war on their corresponding banks of the Boyne. As part of their preparation, William and a few of his men went out to survey the banks to find suitable points to cross the water. While out on this reconnaissance, William received a bullet to the shoulder from the opposite side of the river. The wound was deep, but in a place were it would not be fatal. The King of England had been lucky, had the bullet struck him a few inches in either direction William, King of England, Ireland and Scotland and stadholder of Orange, could have died and history would have been very different. William's injury is recorded in an account made by the Williamite chaplain, George Story:

> Their gunners fired a piece which killed us two horses and a man about one hundred yards above where he king was. But immediately comes a second which had almost

been a fatal one for it grazed upon the bank of the river and in the raising slanted upon the king's right shoulder, took a piece out of his coat and tore the skin and flesh.

('A true and impartial history of the most material occurrences in the Kingdom of Ireland during the two last years' Story p.75)

After his wound was dressed, William and his council of war continued making plans that evening. A big contrast to how James had reacted to a nose bleed two years previously. After much debate they decided the best place for the major part of the battle to unfold was near a spot known as Oldbridge. The Jacobites on the southern bank would be vulnerable there and open to attack from both sides. It was also decided that the Williamites should wear greenery on their uniforms, in order to identify friend from foe in the heat of the battle.

Before the main battle the Williamites, planned on setting a diversion at Oldbridge so that the main battle should take James and his Jacobites by surprise and catch them unprepared. At dawn the next day, 1 July 1690, 8,000 men from the Williamite camp marched on foot towards the town of Plane in County Meath. This stealthy manoeuvre was helped by the early morning mist which acted as additional camouflage. This party of 8,000 men were led by William's leading, general Fredrick Schomberg. Schomberg and the men reached a point on the banks of the Boyne known as Rough Grange. From this point they spotted a group of 500 mounted Jacobites. Within minutes the Jacobites had attempted to cross the ford to attack, but luck was on the Protestant side as the river was too deep and fast for their horses to cross at this point. The Jacobites were forced to return to the south bank and as they retreated the Williamites were able to fire at and wound them from the northern bank. This started the diversionary fighting away from Oldbridge, and the battle had started according

William's plan. James had fallen for the ruse, making one of the biggest mistakes of the battle before it had properly begun. The former king of England had sent his elite French troops after Schomberg's diversion, which was leading James's best soldiers towards a steep boggy valley that was totally unsuitable for hand-to-hand or mounted fighting.

The water flow had reduced enough for the first of the Protestant forces to cross the Boyne and start the main battle at Oldbridge at 08.00. It became clear that the Jacobite council of war had been less comprehensive in their planning than their opposition. The Jacobites might have been less prepared, but they did have a fair number of able men, mounted on good Irish horses, armed with pistols and swords. Theses mounted Jacobites were effective in the early part of the fight and caused an indentation within the French Huguenot contingency of William's army. When William saw this he apparently said: 'My poor guards, my poor guards, my poor guards.' (*Ireland's Fate: The Boyne and After* Shepherd, R. p.107) It was not just William who had seen this disaster unfold, Schomberg had also seen the Huguenot being crushed and decided to go to their aid as he wanted to help and defend his fellow Protestants. Unfortunately he was wounded and killed in his attempt to help them. In turn, the former governor of Derry, George Walker, attempted to help Schomberg and he too lost his life in his attempt.

Even through William had been wounded the day before, he did not shy away from the battle and was in among the hurly burly of the fighting, giving his men directions and commands. He took little care for his own safety, as he proudly wore the star and garter which marked him out as James's usurper – and an easy target for the Jacobites. This disregard for his personal safety continued into the battle:

> His majesty was here in the crowd of all, drawing his sword and animating those that fled to follow him. His danger was great among the enemy's guns which killed

thirty of the Enniskillingers on the spot. Nay one of the Enniskillingers came with a pistol cocked to his majesty till he [William] called out What, are you angry with your friends?'

(*Ireland's Fate: The Boyne and After*
Shepherd, R. p.115)

At midday William commanded that Godert de Ginkell, another of his very able generals, take his men east along the northern bank of the river, to find a more suitable crossing point. This search was successful and an appropriate point near Drybridge was where William finally crossed the River Boyne. Legend has it that while he was crossing the river his horse got stuck, causing the king to dismount. While wading in the water, it is said that William suffered one of his reoccurring asthma attacks. If this legend is true then this did not stop the new king for long. Once on dry land he recovered swiftly and remounted his freed horse to enter the battle on the south bank. It was William who led a side-on attack at the Jacobites causing them to move back towards Donore. During this part of the battle, James's illegitimate son, James FitzJames, Duke of Berwick, was in the thick of the fight and was extremely lucky to survive the ensuing mayhem.

The Jacobites were starting to grow desperate. They continued to fight but were eventually ordered to retreat in the mid-afternoon. The common men that had made up most of the Jacobite fighters, started to flee the battle in fear, disregarding valuable items such as coats, shoes and weapons in an effort to be able to run faster. They also hoped that if spotted by the enemy they would not be taken for soldiers. These men must have been desperate, clothing, shoes and weapons, although heavy, were valuable and worth a lot to a peasant farmer or a labourer. Those who were spotted were shown no mercy by the victorious Williamites, who shot them down like coney rabbits in a field. Again the Williamite chaplain George Story witnessed this behaviour: 'Few or none of the men escaped that came in their hands. For they shot them like hares among the corn and in the hedges as they found them in their march.' (Story, G. pp.84-5)

As his men retreated and fled for their lives, James too fled from the battle scene. He and a small retinue of guards escaped by crossing the River Nanny where it flowed through the Meath town of Duleek. From here the party rode to Duncannon, a port near Waterford, where James caught a ship and returned to exile in France. He did not bring Berwick back to France with him, Berwick instead stayed on to take command and lead the Jacobites instead of his father.

James's escape is recorded in Lord Viscount Sidney's witness account of the Williamite wars: 'Some say that King James sent Sir Patrick Trans and another gentleman towards Waterford to provide shipping for him beforehand, for fear of the worst but I have not heard the certainty of it.' (*A true and impartial history...* p.88) There is debate as to whether William allowed his father-in-law to flee the battle unscathed for the sake of his wife Mary. Given that James was able to escape his guards and get to the Kent coast in late 1688 there is a high probability that he did in fact allow him to escape alive once again, but of course we will never know for sure. William and his victorious army continued on to Dublin while the remaining Jacobites moved to Limerick in the south to set up their new headquarters, minus their champion and figurehead James. The Jacobites had congregated the south of Ireland in and around the city of Sligo so they could be within easy reach of any southern ports. They still over-optimistically hoped that James II and Louis XIV would send more aid to them and their cause.

The two sides were not evenly matched in size or experience and the death tolls of the battle reflect this. It is estimated that 50,000 souls fought in the battle and the fighting raged for four bloody hours. About 2,000 died, of which about 800 were Williamites. Although they were the winning side with fewer deaths, the Williamites did sustain a higher number of wounded men. Unfortunately, the battle did not draw this grudge match to a close as the war in Ireland would continue for a further fifteen months.

In June 1691 the Williamites besieged the town of Athlone. Situated on the banks of the river Shannon, and within territory held by the Jacobites, Ginkell and his men knew it was important to dislodge the Jacobites and create a Williamite position within the strong Jacobite territory. This was not the first attempt by the Williamites to take the town and this time they had a score to settle. The siege started on 20 June, and the first wave of the assault forced the Jacobites to cross the Shannon to the river's west bank. In order to halt the enemy in their tracks, the Jacobites destroyed a crossing bridge after they used it. By doing this, the Jacobites would strike a major blow to their own side. One of their senior commanders, Colonel Grace was killed by accident as they destroyed the bridge. Initially the Jacobites managed to keep Ginkell and his men away. Having learnt from their previous failed attempt at capturing Athlone, the Williamites came prepared with suitable weapons. Utilising these weapons the Protestants assaulted the town using cannon, mortar fire and bombs with no let up in the attack which continued for ten days.

The siege would come to an end after a lucky break. Ginkell spotted a point on the river where he thought it might be possible to ford. If it proved safe, his men could access the Jacobites and defeat them. He tested to see if it was safe by using three men who had been convicted of cowardice forcing them to try to get across. The prisoners proved the point was safe and Ginkell was able to send over 2,000 men to attack the Jacobites from behind. The fighting only lasted ninety minutes before the Jacobites retreated. Ginkell had won the town of Athlone and a toe hold in Jacobite territory.

The majority of the victorious Williamites now continued towards the south west of Ireland and on to what would become the bloodiest battle of the Williamite war. It was now the summer of 1691 and on 12 July 1691, both sides came face to face once again. This time it was near the small village of Aughrim in county Galway. The two sides both had about 20,000 men, but just as in the previous events of this conflict the Williamites were the better trained and more experienced of the two sides, giving them a bigger advantage – although it is worth noting at the beginning of the battle it was the Jacobites who held the strategic advantage. Under the leadership of the Frenchman Charles Chalmot de Saint-Ruhe and supported by the Chevalier de Tessé, John Hamilton, William Dorrington and Patrick Sarsfield, the Jacobites found themselves at the top of a ridge known as Kilcommadan Hill, giving them the advantage of height. They also found themselves protected by boggy and waterlogged land with only one easy access way for the Williamites to attack them, making it easier to defend, in theory. Story noted the battle site and the advantages to the Jacobites in his eyewitness account of the battle:

> M. Saint-Ruth [Ruhe] in making choice of such a piece of ground as nature itself could not furnish him with better, considering all circumstances; for he knew that the Irish naturally loved a breastwork between them and bullets, and here they were fitted to the purpose with hedges and ditches to the very edge of the bog.

> (Story, G. p.122)

The Williamites were still under the steady command of Godert de Ginkell. During the battle a Scottish officer, Hugh Mackay, who had links to the Netherlands, also played an important and decisive role within the battle. Other leading figures within the Williamite commanders were Henri de Massue a French Huguenot and Thomas Tollemache, who was the Colonel of the Coldstream Guards. It was the Williamites who opened the battle at 14.00. By 16.00 they were forced to retreat to safety and hold a council of war. Ginkell argued that they should pause conflict until the following day, but Hugh Mackay countered his superior's argument saying that now opening fire had been exchanged, the Williamites should continue with the attack. Mackay won out and ninety minutes later William's men were back out in the action fighting through the boggy cold waters, often thigh deep and attacking upwards to try and get to the Jacobites. Unsurprisingly, they suffered heavy losses and retreated back again.

The next plan of attack from the Williamites was that they would try to access the Jacobites via the lower land using mounted cavalrymen. This plan was flawed too as it left many of these men vulnerable to the enemy; there was no shelter from the bullets of the Jacobites. During this part of the attack some of the Williamite cannons were also damaged, but luck changed when William's Protestants were able to hold land close to a local ruined castle. By taking this ruin the Williamite mounted soldiers were protected as they crossed the causeway more safely than before. The Jacobites who had been protecting the rundown ruin retreated when they saw the number of armed enemies approaching. This was an important turning point in the battle.

Fate then issued the Jacobites a cruel blow. Around 20.00, after six hours of fighting and as dusk was falling on the battle, Charles Chalmot de Saint-Ruhe was decapitated by a cannonball. The Jacobites had just lost their most competent commander. George Story noted of Saint-Ruhe's death: '[he was] killed with a great shot from one of our batteries'. The inexperienced fighting men, tired from hours of fighting and now without a leader, started to flee into the night in fear. The Jacobites inexperience and lack of leadership lost them the bloody battle. Of course the Williamites took full advantage of the ensuing chaos, utilising their discipline, training and experience over the less experienced Jacobites. Just like the end of the Battle of the Boyne, the Williamites attacked those Jacobites in flight for their lives. Accusations of cruelty and violence were aimed at by both sides in the aftermath the battle. These accusations were related to how each side supposedly treated their captured prisoners. Tensions and feeling were high during this battle and Aughrim was by far the bloodiest of all the battles and skirmishes of the Williamite war in Ireland. The exact figures for the number of men who lost their lives in the seven-hour battle is not known, but it is estimated that between

5,000–7,000 souls died on the battlefield, with the majority of losses going to the Jacobite cause.

The Battle of Aughrim would be the last face-to-face battle of the war, but it was not the last event of the war, even though it was obvious by this stage that the war was all but won by the Williamites. The Jacobites, ever hopeful, insisted on still holding out hope that James, backed by Louis of France, would send additional help. The south had been dominated by the Jacobites for the majority of the Williamite war and they had made their base in the city of Limerick, which would become the last target and the climax of the Williamite war. To this end, Ginkell and the Williamites had attempted to take the city in August 1690, but the Jacobites had kept the city that time. This time Ginkell was determined to finish the job by taking advantage of the Jacobites' low morale after losing at the bloody battle of Aughrim the previous month.

In truth it was James's old pal Tyrconnell who was the most optimistically delusional that the Jacobites could keep the Williamites out of Limerick, so when this last stoic believer suffered a series of strokes which first lost him the ability to communicate, and then his life on 14 September 1691, it was little wonder that the Jacobites sought to negotiate fairly swiftly. Unlike Derry at the beginning of the war, Limerick had a good supply of food as the bombardment of the city started, but it seems both sides were now weary of this campaign. For the Williamites wanted to be back on mainland Europe and fighting in the main events of the Nine Years' War. Any subsequent skirmishes or battles were both distracting and expensive to continue. The Jacobites knew they had lost and did not want to spend another winter in Ireland. Therefore, despite the fact that the attacks on the city were nowhere near as intense as the bombardment at Athlone, it was the Jacobites that sought to start negotiations for peace – not just for the city of Limerick, but to end the war. There was also a danger if peace on the Irish front was not reached soon, then the grudge match between the Irish Catholics and the settled Protestants on Irish soil could have continued indefinitely. To a degree it did, and the

Williamite war's legacy would last well into the twentieth century, causing thousands of other deaths over religious doctrines and who rightfully ruled the isle of Ireland.

After the Siege of Limerick, peace negotiations started fairly swiftly. The two sides were not represented by James or William in person but by trusted military men on both sides. James's spokesperson at the peace agreement was Patrick Sarsfield. Ironically, Sarsfield had started his military career when he was recruited to a regiment of soldiers under the leadership of the Duke of Monmouth in the Anglo-Dutch wars during the reign of Charles II. After Charles's death and James's accession, Sarsfield did not remain loyal to his old military leader, instead choosing to help the king James defeat Monmouth's ill-fated rebellion. Sarsfield, like James, was a Catholic and would be come important to the Jacobite cause. James bestowed him with the title of 1st Earl of Lucan and he was part of the party that arrived on Irish soil with James in March 1689. He would become a member of the Patriot Parliament established by James. He was, therefore, a skilled and experienced soldier and statesman and ideal for the task of negotiating peace and ensuring the safe removal of the remaining Jacobites from the Irish front.

Sarsfield's opposition, and William's representative in the peace treaty talks was General Godert de Ginkell. He too had had an active military career before the Williamite war, having fought during the Franco-Dutch wars. In 1688 he was part of the invasion party who accompanied William to England in the Glorious Revolution. He also accompanied William to Ireland in 1690 where he was active in leading the Dutch mounted fighters in the Battle of the Boyne. He stayed on in Ireland and led the Dutch troop in the bloodier battle of Aughrim. The treaty negotiated that the two sides comprised of two parts; the first dealt with military, primarily in ending the fighting and fairly dealing with the groups of fighting men still on the isle of Ireland. This part of the negotiations was far easier for the men involved to agree on, as they were pragmatic military men who had other battles to fight. It was less easy to find compromises in the second part of the negotiations. This part of the negotiations dealt with the civil rights, faith and property in this the new chapter of Irish history under William and Mary's reign.

The civil terms were not popular among the Protestants, but they were upheld. The men of the Jacobite forces were given three options: option one was to continue to serve James II and the Jacobites in France. It is estimated that 14,000 men took up this offer, many bringing their wives and families with them. They left Ireland from the port city of Cork for France. Option two was to defect to the Williamite army and remain in Ireland as soldiers. For these men, a wage was a wage and fighting was their occupation. They did not fight for a cause and they also did not want to leave their homeland. Around 1,000 men chose this as their option. The last choice was to leave the army altogether and return to their homes to start a new career path. Approximately 2,500 men did this, laying down their arms and swearing loyalty to their new monarchs. However, the men who chose the last two options would never be fully trusted and this created suspicion and tension within communities. It is worth mentioning that although a conservative estimate of 75 per cent of the population identified as Catholic in Ireland at the time of the Glorious Revolution and the beginning of the Williamite war, the majority of these people were everyday tenants who rented and worked the land for their landlords. Life did not change for them whether their overlords were Irish Catholic or Anglo Protestant, they still needed to pay rent, feed their family and work the land. In this case, when referring to Catholics within the terms of the treaty it is to the landed classes, not the working majority.

Striking a deal with William had also become more palatable for the Irish Catholics in 1691 because he was part of the Catholic League of Augsburg, which was allied with the papacy despite the fact that he was Protestant. In Europe, William worked with Austria and England's former enemy, Catholic Spain, in his efforts to stand up to Louis XIV's French forces. The papal support did not last long as just two years later in 1693, the Pope changed allegiance and decided to recognise James II and not William as the rightful King of Ireland – at this point, the whole of Ireland was ruled by the British throne. William was not only king of Britain, but ruler of Orange in the Netherlands and still engaged in a war with Louis XIV on the continent, and therefore could not spend excessive amounts of time in Ireland controlling the population. The Catholic gentry of Ireland were expected to sign an oath of loyalty to William and Mary, despite them being Protestant, as an important assurance that they, rather than the throne-less James II, were accepted as the monarchs of Ireland. It was hoped that by doing this, the people of Ireland would remain loyal to William should James try to invade again.

The Protestant settlers who called Ireland their home felt that these terms were unacceptable and too lenient on the Catholics, even through they, the Protestants, were the minority. This was why, unlike the military settlement, the terms of the civil agreement were not kept. The treaty soon became known as the 'Broken Treaty' in Catholic circles. Many of the landed Irish Catholics would still go on and lose their land even after swearing the required oath. By the end of 1691, only 5 per cent of the land in Ireland was still in Catholic ownership. That was lower than the period after Cromwell had finished causing havoc in the 1650s.

The Williamite war was the result of years of Irish Catholic repression from the English, even before the English Reformation. Before then it was an 'English' problem rather than a 'Protestant' problem. The tensions were then reawakened by the cruelty of Cromwell during the interregnum. These events had taken place within the living memory of many when the Williamite war broke out in late 1688 – early 1689. The war would have many consequences in Ireland, Britain, Europe, and directly for the future of James II, as well as igniting those long-held tensions that would continue to cause violence over centuries and eventually explode and boil over into paramilitary fighting in the early twentieth century and again during The Troubles in the later part of the same century.

For the people of Ireland, the Battle of the Boyne and the Siege of Derry both still live in the collective memory and still evoke passions, even after the Good Friday Agreement. Unlike the civil part of the Treaty of Limerick, the 1998 Good Friday Agreement has managed to bring reconciliation and accord to Ireland. The old passions still lay under the surface and are displayed annually during the marching season, when the apprentice boys of Derry and the Battle of the Boyne are remembered. The Williamite war did not start the tensions in Ireland, it had been a tinderbox waiting to ignite due to British colonialism.

For William and Mary, the war helped seal their positions as joint monarchs, even if it had been an expensive distraction from the Nine Years' War that had always been the bigger priority for William. Williamite victory in Ireland must have had a reaffirming and morale boosting effect on the people of Britain – a divine sign that William was indeed 'God approved' to be their monarch rather than James. In the bigger European picture, the Williamite victory in Ireland would also have been a morale boost for William and his anti-French league. It had briefly put Ireland centre of the European stage and history. It had been a consequence of the Glorious Revolution, but it had given William and his allies more resources in their crusade against Louis XIV and stopping French imperialism.

The saddest consequences were for James II. The ramifications were both political and personal for the former king. After escaping in the aftermath of the Battle of the Boyne, James never returned to his former kingdoms. The Jacobites, as we saw, continued in vain to try and secure Ireland for him to try and regain his other thrones, but it was not possible against William, his allies and resources. The Jacobite plotting and planning did not stop with the Irish war. James's new home at the chateau of St Germain des pres, became the headquarters for the Jacobite cause, where the focus shifted from James, to that of his son, James Francis Edward Stuart, lately known as The Old Pretender.

At 57 years old James was no longer a young man and with his military background he must have realised that it would not be possible to win against William, the Protestant British military and the resources William had in Europe. The war in Ireland had proved it to him. This must have been personally very disappointing. He had followed in his father's footsteps, he had lost his thrones. He had lost everything his brother Charles II had rebuilt after the Restoration; the only consolation was that he had not followed in the family tradition of losing his head in the process.

Exile and Death 1691–1701

Immediately after the Jacobites defeat at the Battle of the Boyne, in the summer of 1690, James fled to the Irish coast and returned back to France. This was not the result either he or his host, Louis XIV, had wanted. While James's queen, Mary of Modena must have been relieved that her husband had not been killed in his failed attempts to regain the thrones of his lost kingdoms, she also must have wondered, like James, what their futures would hold now he had been unable to achieve his goals in Ireland. Prior to leaving for the Irish campaign, James, in his characteristic egotistical arrogance, had employed a historian to record his 'victories'. Now, upon his return, the poor academic found himself unemployed rather than recording great historical events from an important eyewitness for all prosperity. (*James II: King in Exile* Callow, J. p.187) James's arrival back in Normandy confused many French observers. For they believed that James and his Jacobites had triumphed in Ireland and even killed his son-in-law William during the infamous Battle of the Boyne.

James returned to what would be his home for the rest of his lifetime, the rundown and once grand, Chateau of Saint-Germain-en-Laye in the outskirts of the city of Paris. Soon after returning from Ireland, Louis came to St Germain to meet with his dethroned cousin. If James was expecting Louis to supply more men and money to continue with his uphill challenge to try and regain his crown and kingdoms, then he was going to be greatly disappointed at the meeting. Instead James meet a cool reception from his royal cousin, the French monarch refused to support or commit to anything proposed by James until he fully understood situation in Ireland. Wisely, Louis was unwilling to throw good money after bad, especially given he was also fighting a

European war at the time. The French king departed Saint-Germain-en-Laye as quickly as he had arrived to return to Versailles.

This perceived rejection from Louis caused James to grow desperate. He pestered his cousin with a stream of missives begging him for further help in getting his thrones back. But this method of approach did not work with the Sun King. In short, Louis spurned James – and he was not the only person to reproach him. His queen and wife, Mary of Modena, may have been glad that her husband had returned from war in one piece, but she would chastise her husband and remind him of his failures. This discord between the two did not last long; by late 1691, Mary of Modena was once again pregnant.

James now had two choices open to him: seek alliance and support elsewhere, or accept the position he now found himself in and live under the generous patronage of his cousin in France. He was 57 years of age and although today 57 is perceived as still relatively young, by seventeenth-century standards he was considered somewhat of a veteran and no longer young. Wisely, James chose to accept his new fate and started to settle down to making a new life in France. He took to riding around the grounds, countryside and wooded lands in and around the town of Saint-Germain-en-Laye. He also demonstrated this acceptance through making previously temporary posts at Saint-Germain-en-Laye permanent. Through this act, James was non-verbally and indirectly telling the court that he no longer expected to relocate back to London in the position of victorious restored monarch. He also established a small cabinet of advisors, again sending out the clear message that he was settling into his new life in exile. The cabinet was made up of four men: John Caryll, secretary to Queen Mary of Modena; Sir Richard Nagle, who oversaw 'Affairs of the Nation'; Father Louis Innes, who advised James on Scottish matters; and Lord Melfort, who held the post of Secretary of State.

This new acceptance of his predicament did not stop the Jacobite cause. The Williamite war continued for over a year in Ireland after the Jacobites were defeated at the Battle of Boyne; when peace was finally made and the war had ended, many of the former Jacobite troops made their way to France. Under the terms of the treaty of Limerick, all men who fought for the Jacobites, whether French or Irish, were granted safe passage to France and many of the Irish who had fought took up the offer. This men where known as the Wild Geese. When the war ended in 1691, Louis's attitude to James thawed and the French king was once again more amenable to discuss plans for the future. The Wild Geese and Louis's renewed interest caused James to once again see new hope that he may yet get his thrones back.

In December 1691, James relocated himself to the Breton city of Nantes. The purpose of which was so that he could be on the spot as the troops from Ireland arrived. The arrival of so many men willing to help his cause must have been a boost to James's dented ego and personal confidence. Further to seeing physical evidence of renewed support, James had started to receive correspondence from John Churchill, now the Earl of Marlborough. Marlborough it seems was keeping his options open as William had failed to reward him as Marlborough had expected after his bravery and service in Ireland. William never really trusted Marlborough's loyalty because of his former alliance to his father-in-law.

Marlborough was not his only correspondent either. His estranged daughter, Princess Anne (later Queen Anne), had also reached out to her father, asking him to forgive her for her behaviour in 1688. Anne was close to Marlborough's wife Sarah – how close is up for debate, and it may have been Sarah's influence that encouraged Anne to re-establish relations with her exiled father.

Things on British soil were not all harmonious. Relations between James's daughters, Queen Mary, and Princess Anne was fraught with tension. The main cause being the Churchills. These tensions coincided with the ending of William and Mary's honeymoon on the throne after the events of the Glorious Revolution. Although William was of the correct religious denomination, he was – in British eyes – 'foreign', despite the fact his mother had been a Stuart and he was ruling with his English Stuart wife.

Equally, James and his Jacobite cause were not without supporters in London – and not just Catholic supporters. From late 1690, a group of Jacobite sympathisers who were of Protestant faith met in Covent Garden, London. Among these supporters were: William Penn the Younger – the son of the founder of the US State Pennsylvania, John Ashton – who had acted as Mary of Modena's clerk; and Louis de Durford, 2nd Earl of Feversham – a French Huguenot who had supported James after his accession to the throne, and had even helped put down the Monmouth rebellion. It is easy to see why James was once more optimistic.

When news of James's relocation to Nantes reached London, rumours started to circulate within the city that they may find themselves invaded once again. John Evelyn, a seventeenth-century diarist and contemporary of the gossiping Samuel Pepys, wrote 'reports of an invasion ... alarmed the city, court and people', (Evelyn, J. 1691) William did not rest on his laurels and decided not to take any chances in case these rumours were true. The new monarch rounded up all of the influential suspected and well known pro-Jacobites, and detained them, at his royal pleasure, in the infamous Tower of London. Among those who William placed in the Tower was John Churchill, Earl of Marlborough. The fact that Marlborough had been corresponding with James proves William was right to have been weary of the earl.

In early 1692, James once again found that he was in a position to regain his crown. But true to form, it was James himself who would destroy any chance of this happening by issuing a declaration, dated 20 April 1692, which was circulated around London. This long declaration was little more than a diatribe blaming his former subjects for his current situation and woes:

> Through an affair of this nature speaks for itself, nor do
> we think ourselves obliged to say any thing more on this
> occasion than that we come to assert our own just rights
> and deliver our people from oppression.

(*The life of James II* Stanier-Clarke, J.)

There is more than a hint of irony to this, because the main reason that the Glorious Revolution took place was that James was becoming increasingly autocratic and oppressive. The pompous tone then turned accusatory with blame aimed towards his former subjects, suggesting that they were stupid and easily fooled by William. 'Many of our subjects were cheated into the late revolution by the arts of ill men particularly the Prince of Orange's declaration.' (*The life of James II* Stanier-Clarke, J.). He then goes on to refer to the Glorious Revolution and the Williamite War in Ireland as a 'quarrel', and that 'English blood ... [was] unnecessarily trifled away in this quarrel'. If you want to win over your former subjects, it would be much better to demonstrate that you have changed, that you are going to show mercy and empathy, and this ill-advised declaration seems to be doing the exact opposite.

Further down the declaration it gets even worse. James actually names people with whom he wants to settle scores with once he is king again:

> We do hereby declare and promise on the word of a king that all persons whatsoever, how guilty so ever they may have been (except the persons following: The Duke of Armanda, Marquis of Winchester, Earl of Sunderland, Earl of Danby, Earl of Nottingham...) otherwise considered and rewarded by us as the merit of the case shall require.

(*The life of James II* Stanier-Clarke, J.)

The list partially quotes some of the people with whom James wanted to settle scores and this list included bishops, gentry and the jurors that found John Ashton guilty, and sent Ashton subsequently to the hangman. Ashton had been the go-between for the court in Saint-Germain-en-Laye and the Covent Garden Jacobites.

In short, the declaration was a long-winded, bitter, pompous, blame-shifting, arrogant and over bearing mistake. William was in his other territories at the time, but Mary, James's own daughter, used this declaration to cause the greatest damage to her father's reputation, ensuring it was widely circulated and so promoting her and William's popularity, and solidifying suspicion and mistrust towards her father. James had learnt nothing of his or his father's previous mistakes; his arrogance had blinded him to it. He was his father's son through and through.

Prior to sending his declaration over to English shores, James had started to prepare to invade Britain in a seventeenth-century Jacobite Armada during April 1692. James met with his illegitimate son, Berwick, in Normandy along with the French marshal, de Bellefonds. These men set about discussing their naval plans for the avenging Jacobite Armada. These over-ambitious plans were soon brought to a pause, when spring storms in the harbour of La Havre scuppered and damaged many of James's fleet of borrowed French ships.

James was also expecting more vessels to join his invading force from the direction of the Mediterranean. This fleet had been delayed as it had encountered problems off the coast of North Africa. The additional fleet's journey should have taken them around Spain, past Portugal and up north to the Normandy coast, but the weather was fighting against James's plans; he should have taken this as a bad omen and aborted his plans. Mistakenly, in May, James and his Jacobite supporters glimpsed a sliver of hope when they spotted some ships. They were only a small portion of the vessels that James had been expecting to help carry out his plans of invading England. However, the size of the fleet would not be his downfall.

This small fleet of eighty-eight ships spotted by James were being led by Captain Edward Russell, later to be made 1st Earl of Orford. Russell had been communicating with James at St Germain prior to 1692; however, as he sailed these ships towards James and his Jacobite cause, Russell chose to change sides and defected to the Williamites. This change of heart and loyalty is most likely due to the content of James's declaration, published the previous month. By changing his loyalty, the Jacobites found themselves out numbered 2:1. The subsequent sea battles between the English and Dutch Williamites against the French and Irish Jacobites, which took place off the coast of Normandy, became known as the Battles of Barfleur and La Hougue.

The two fleets saw each other off the coast of Barfleur, Normandy, at 06.00 on 29 May 1692. Engagement between the French Jacobites and the joint English and Dutch Williamites did not start until 10.00. By 11.00 the two sides were continually attacking each other. The French had managed to retreat to some shelter but by 20.00 the British took advantage of this and deployed fireships to cause maximum destruction to the anchored and sheltered vessels. The following day the remaining French ships cut anchor and moved off away from the Normandy coast and during the following fortnight there were skirmishes between the two sides. In early June, Queen Mary received news from the channel and it is recorded in the state papers 'Whitehall. The queen ... understands that the fleet was off Cape de Hogue ... pursuing the enemy she requires that person addressed join the fleet under Admiral Russell with all expedition.' (CSP Dom Hardy W&M 1691–1692 p.295) By 14 June 1692, the Williamites had destroyed the majority of the Jacobite French fleet. England was safe from another Catholic Armada.

This was a sad situation for James to find himself in. During his brother Charles's reign, he had been the admiral of the British Royal Navy – for him to fail via an attempted sea invasion must have stung. Even after it was obvious that the there was nothing left for him to do, James had not released the troops amassed off the Normandy coast or returned to St Germain. Was he clinging on to last hope, knowing deep down that once he went back to the suburbs of Paris, that his military and naval careers would be over and that he was unlikely to have another opportunity to attempt to get his thrones back. In all probability, given his mental state since 1688, this is the likely reason for his delaying. Eventually, it was Louis who sent orders to the camp, he commanded that the troops there be redeployed to various front lines as France was still fighting several fronts in the Nine Years' War. This was a very public rejection from his cousin Louis. Four days after he arrived back from the Normandy coast, on 28 June 1692, Mary of Modena gave birth to a daughter, Princess Louise Marie Stuart.

James's life at Saint-Germain-en-Laye quickly fell in to a routine. He was a creature of habit rising between 07.00 and 07.30 each morning. His days were filled with riding, hunting, walking, reading, any business of his 'states' with his small privy cabinet of advisors, and entertaining visitors. Among the animals he was able to hunt within the woodland and countryside surrounding his borrowed chateau at St Germain were foxes, deer, waterfowl and even wolves. He had become a true gentleman of leisure.

Although the chateau of Saint-Germain-en-Laye was not in great condition when Louis loaned it to James, the former king and queen did not renovate or restore the palace they called home for the last part of their lives. This was understandable as finances were tight and they were only leasing the chateau. It was somewhat ironic that the chateau's fading grandeur mirrored this last period of James's life.

It was from this point onwards that the focus of the exiled Jacobean court changed from James II to that of his youngest son, Prince James Francis Edward. This change was particularly seen after 1695 when the young prince had his own household created within St Germain, under the presumptuous title of The Household of the Prince of Wales. The royal title of Prince of Wales was then, as it is today, the title bestowed upon the eldest legitimate son and heir apparent to the British throne. As James was no longer the British king, and his second daughter from his first wife, Princess Anne, was Britain's heir apparent in 1695 (Mary II had died the previous year with no issue or heirs from her marriage to William III), it was somewhat over-confident of James and Mary of Modena to give their son this title. As the little Prince had been brought up in the Roman Catholic faith, James should have realised that the people of his former kingdoms of

Great Britain and Ireland would never again accept a Catholic as their monarch – although this attitude is typical of James's pompous and self-important character. This is also reflected in James's opinions, views and behaviours, none which had changed in this last exile, particularly his notions and belief in the Divine Rights of Kings. This is not surprising in some ways, as he was the guest of the living embodiment of this belief, Louis XIV, the Sun king.

In this, the last exile of his life, James's religious conviction to the Catholic church and heightened sense of morality grew even stronger, the way many religious converts' convictions strengthen over time. This is evident in his rationalising of why he had 'failed'. Instead of taking responsibility for actions, James reasoned that all his failures were due to his previous 'sinful' life, particularly while a promiscuous young man during his youth during the Interregnum and during his brother's reign and his first marriage to Anne Hyde. He believed this so firmly that he was determined his son, the young Prince of Wales, would not follow in his father's or late Uncle Charles's fornicating footsteps. This is of course an absurd notion. For his father, Charles I, who had also failed as king, was devoted to his wife, James's mother Henrietta Maria. While at the extreme opposite end of the morality scale – according to James's thinking – was his brother Charles II, who has gone down in history for his libertine lifestyle and was arguably far more successful a monarch than either his father or bother – he managed to remain king until his death and to die in his bed of natural causes.

James was not just worried about his son's moral and spiritual wellbeing, but also for the young prince's education. This might have been due to the fact that James himself had had an intermittent and patchy education due to the Civil Wars of his childhood. By the time he was exiled in Europe he was old enough to seek adventure and fight as solider, a far more appealing opportunity than studying. Therefore, in a similar manner to the much later Queen Victoria, the young Prince of Wales found himself living in a household dominated by 'rules' dictated by his father, that were set out within documents James had written in 1692 and 1696.

James's youngest daughter Princess Louise Marie, born in exile in 1692 after the disastrous Battles of Barfleur and La Hougue, had a much less rigorous upbringing and education. Sadly she never reached her full potential as she contracted smallpox and subsequently died on 28 April 1712, eleven years after her father's death. She was just shy of her twentieth birthday.

James's illegitimate children also made up part of the exiled Jacobean court at Saint-Germain-en-Laye. They, like their half siblings Mary and Anne, did not live up to the high moral standards James expected of both his court and children during the later part of his life. His three children with Arabella Churchill (sister to John Churchill, later Earl of Marlborough), are prime examples of young spirited Stuarts with a lust – in all senses of the word – for life.

James FitzJames, Duke of Berwick, who fought in Ireland for his father's cause, married the widow of the Jacobite general Patrick Sarsfield. Sarsfield had help to negotiate the Treaty of Limerick. His young widow, Lady Honora, was only 19 years old when her husband died and was expecting his child at the time of his death. Berwick married Lady Honora in 1695, and raised Sarsfield's child as his own. But it was not happy ever after just yet for Berwick. Lady Honora died of consumption on 16 January 1698, leaving her husband a widower at 28 years old. He remarried again, two years later to a woman of lower status – Anne Bulkeley, the daughter of James's Master of the Household at Saint-Germain-en-Laye. Given that Berwick was illegitimate himself, the difference in their status was less of an issue, but still scandalous enough.

The second of his illegitimate sons by Arabella Churchill was Henry FitzJames, Duke of Albemarle. Albemarle was little more than a wastrel and a drunk with a reputation for being 'the stupidest man on Earth', (*James II: King in Exile* Callow, J. p.359) and like many of his ilk lived hard and died young aged 29. He too fell rather short of his father's high moral standards.

But it was his illegitimate daughter Henrietta that would be the most scandalous of his natural children. When James returned defeated from Ireland after the Battle of the Boyne, he arrived back to find a newly widowed Henrietta. She was only 20 years old. The pious atmosphere James attempted to create at Saint-Germain-en-Laye was insular and confining to the young woman, so she set about finding a way to entertain herself. Henrietta's entertainment came in the form of an Irish brigadier and former MP for Belfast, Mark Talbot. He was part of the 'Wild Geese' who had migrated to James's Jacobean court in France after the Treaty of Limerick. The pair's scandalous liaison unfortunately did not end in marriage as Talbot was accused of expressing less than charitable opinions about James while under the influence of drink. Subsequently he found himself degraded from the French army by Louis XIV, and spent time in the notorious French gaol, the Bastille. Considering the scandal, Henrietta was extremely lucky to eventually marry in 1695. Her second husband was the Earl of Newcastle, Piers Butler, and she remained married to him until her death in 1730.

James's eldest natural children, both the legitimate Mary and Anne as well as his illegitimate including Berwick, Albemarle and lady Henrietta, were far from perfect examples of the pious, obedient and moral children expected by the former king. James's fevered religiosity and faith in his later years more than made up for what he perceived to be their shortcomings in faith. Indeed, reflecting upon the perceived personal shortcomings of his youth may have caused James to embrace his devotions even more strongly. The thoughts of mortality that come with getting older, as well as his perceived military and naval failings after the Boyne and the Battles of Barfleur and La Hougue, may have exasperated his religious conviction.

This fevered conviction caused James to believe that the Reformation under Henry VIII was not only morally wrong but also unlawful, as he firmly believed there was no evidence within the scriptures for the arguments reformists use to defend their beliefs. He was unable to comprehend or conceive why anyone, but especially his former subjects, did not see this and believe as he did. It is this exact attitude, of arrogance with a lack of empathy, that is one of the biggest reasons James failed as monarch. The concept of compromise was not within his nature and he was unwilling to consider it due to the stubbornness of his personality. He was especially unwilling to compromise in important topics such as religion, politics and the institution of monarchy – regardless of how outdated or unpopular his fixed views and opinions may be to others.

The former king had also taken to wearing a penitence belt around his upper thigh. This small spiky belt, worn tight to the skin so the spikes cut into the wearer's flesh, was a popular form of self-punishment used by the very devoted during the sixteenth and seventeenth centuries. The pain inflicted is supposed to atone for the wearer's sins, both new and old. Had James been born and subsequently taken the Crown 150 years earlier, he may well have become one of the most successful monarchs of Great Britain rather than one of our least effective rulers; he was simply born in the wrong time. Also during this time, James justified all the actions he took, whether successful or not, on his religious conviction; if it was unsuccessful, he was making those choices and failing – but doing it because he felt it was the right and moral thing to do. As the old saying goes, being right is not always easy or popular. For example, he justified the Battle of the Boyne and the Irish campaign by claiming he was anointed by God, therefore he was justified in trying to reclaim his throne through war.

This ardent devotion to Roman Catholicism won James admiration and support from Catholic orders such as the Carmelites, Franciscans and Dominican friars. He fed his spiritual needs through visiting French churches and religious houses in his free time. His wife, Mary of Modena, was just as pious as her husband. Although the chateau at Saint-Germain-en-Laye was in poor condition and the royal exile court was low on funds, Mary of Modena found the funds and the justification to renovate her personal private chapel. She was particularly ardent in her devotion and worship of the Sacre

Coeur – the sacred heart of Jesus. This was a small sect that was particularly popular in France during this period. Devotees chose to pray to Jesus's heart as it symbolised his love. Mary of Modena also financially supported the Visitandine order of nuns set up by her late mother-in-law, the dowager queen Henrietta Maria, at nearby La Chaillot. The former queen would take prayer retreats with the Holy sisters and also host them at the chateau. Her connection with their order continued after the death of James in 1701.

James's flamboyant and exaggerated sense of faith and spiritual awakening during the later years of his life in exile allowed him the time to visit La Trappe, a Cistercian abbey based in Normandy in the west of France. At the time of his first of many visits, the abbey was under the its most famous abbot, Armand de Rancé. He was one of the notorious Cardinal Richelieu's godchildren and like James, de Rancé had not always lived a devotional or pious life; he had experienced a similarly debauched youth like James had. Both parties had made a positive impact on each other and James returned annually to the abbey.

In 1698 William tried to unsettle his father-in-law by sending an English ambassador to Versailles and St Germain for six months. The main task of William Bentinck, 1st Earl of Portland, was negotiate with the Sun King about the future of the Spanish monarchy. This was a matter important to both William in his European plans as well as to Louis. On a side mission Bentinck also wanted to cause a rift between Louis and James, to the point that Louis would stop supporting his unfortunate royal cousin with the hopes that he might even expel him from France. This might have been a spiteful act from William in revenge as the Jacobites had an assassination attempt made against the new king two years previously. Both William and his ambassador would have preferred it if James and his supporters were further from his former kingdoms and ideally in Italy. However, Bentinck would fail in that task as Louis remained steadfast and loyal to his unfortunate English cousin; it was a loyalty that was strong right until the end of James's life in 1701.

By 1699 James was regularly suffering from the painful inflection of gout and as a consequence his trips out riding and hunting in the woods and forests surrounding Saint-Germain-en-Laye became less frequent. Then in 1700, James lost his friend Abbot de Rancé and this must have been a personal blow to the exiled king.

* * *

In 1701, Good Friday fell on 4 March. As it is one of the most important dates in the Christian calendar James was of course attending Mass in the private royal chapel in Saint-Germain-en-Laye. While at his devotions and kneeling in prayer, the former king suffered a heavy nose bleed. James had suffered nose bleeds before, most notably at Salisbury Plane when Marlborough deserted him in favour of William. This new episode seems to have been particularly bad; so much so, he collapsed forward in a state of unconsciousness as his nose continued to bleed without stopping. This was the beginning of James's slow decline towards finally meeting his maker. There is something rather fitting about the fact that the start of his mortal end began on Good Friday during mass, especially so for a man who was as pious and religiously devoted as James had become.

Within weeks of this episode, James had started to look as if he was recovering well, appearing as expressive and coherent as before his nose bleed and collapse. Sadly James's recuperation did not last long and within a week of what looked like a tangible recovery, the former king suffered a stroke while at his toilet and getting ready for the day. The aftermath of the stroke was far more serious than the nose bleed, leaving him incapacitated on the right side of his body. When Louis heard of James's sudden stroke, he sent the dauphin's royal medicus to St Germain to treat his cousin. Considering the immediate seriousness of the stroke, within days James was able to write words with his left hand as well walk a little using the aid of a stick; his stubbornness and single-mindedness seemed to help him when he needed these qualities most. Given the period in history and

159

the lack of effective medical remedies and knowledge, this was no small achievement on James's part and he should be admired for his tenacity and persistence.

Although Louis had not always supported James after his military and naval endeavours to regain his throne had failed, the Sun King certainly felt great affection towards his unlucky English cousin, especially in the last months of his life. As well as sending the dauphin's doctor, Louis also sent his own doctor Dr Fagon to Saint-Germain-en-Laye. By the end of March, Fagon felt that James was strong enough to travel to the springs at Bourbon in a litter. Louis was kind enough to provide James with twenty-six of his best horses to get him and his royal entourage to the healing spring waters at Bourbon as safely and as comfortably as possible. He also provided James with 100,000 francs per month for the duration of his time at Bourbon to cover his expenses. The French monarch also wanted James to feel the respect he deserved as an anointed royal king, despite his current circumstances, so while he travelled on his progress towards Bourbon, the French people came out to cheer and wave as the entourage passed slowly through the Loire Valley. Each evening the party stopped at a different religious house, monastery, convent or episcopal palace to rest and see to their devotions. At one point on the journey the party stayed a few days at the convent of Notre Dame La Charité – sur Loire, a convent of the Benedictine order, to give James respite during an acute flare up of his gout.

James was met on this journey by his eldest illegitimate son, the Duke of Berwick. Berwick had been in Italy attempting to gather support and finances for the Jacobean cause when he heard about his father's illness. Once James arrived at Bourbon he underwent a rigorous programme of therapies aimed to help him recover from the stroke, included taking cold baths in the spring waters. During his six week sojourn at the springs James did grow stronger, but whether this was as a direct result of the waters or that he was resting, is hard to know. As he grew stronger the former king slept and ate well; when not taking therapies he was as devoted as ever to his prayers and took to visiting the attached Capuchin monastery and dressing in simple clothes.

The royal party started their return journey to Paris in May 1701. Just before the journey began, James had started to develop stomach aches and to spit up blood, the most likely cause being stomach ulcers. The party stopped at Moulins on the river Allier in the Auvergne-Rhône-Alpes region, situated right in the centre of France. The stop coincided with the feast of Corpus Christi, but much to James's frustration, he was too ill to attend the festivities and Mass for the feast. Just after James and his party returned to St Germain, news from Versailles arrived that James's younger friend and cousin, the Duc d'Orleans, had died of a stroke, aged 60, at his château, Saint-Cloud.

James's last public appearance was on 16 August 1701, when he managed to ride his horse into the nearby forest. The locals of Saint-Germain-en-Laye cheered and waved at him. Twenty-seven days later, on 12 September, James's health took a turn for the worse again. He collapsed while attending Mass. As a consequence of this episode, the former king was given the religious right of Extreme Unction and not expected to survive long. True to nature, right till the end, James was able to surpass all expectations and survive a further four days. During his final days, he took leave of those he loved as he knew that his time on earth was finally drawing to an end. He faced those final days and hours in a state of calm devotion, knowing that he would soon met his saviour.

Recorded in the papers of Sir David Nairne, one of James's chief advisors in exile, James made a new will on the 7 September: 'The new will was read to James II on the following day and signed for him by Lord Middleton before seven witnesses.' (*Sir David Nairne; The life of a Scottish Jacobite at the Court of the Exiled Stuarts* Corp E. p.81)

While waiting for deliverance from this world, James requested to see his youngest children with Mary of Modena, James Francis

Edward and his sister Louise. While saying goodbye to his distraught youngest children, he requested that they remain true to Rome and told little Prince James that he wished that he be known as James III. Two days later, on the 14 September, Louis paid a final visited to his ailing cousin. Both men were emotional when their meeting came to an end and they parted for the final time. Over the next twenty-four hours the former king weakened greatly, before finally breathing his last during the afternoon of 16 September 1701. The final cause of his death has been recorded as being the result of an internal haemorrhage. He had been weeks away from his sixty-eighth birthday.

The late King James II & VII had wanted to be buried in the local church in Saint-Germain-en-Laye with no pomp or fuss, but befitting his former status as king. Louis decided to ignore his cousin's wishes (part of me thinks James would have privately liked that the French king had disregarded this wish). However it was not as straightforward as holding a funeral Mass. First, James's heart was removed and placed in a silver reliquary and bequeathed to the local convent at La Chaillot – the order of nuns established by his mother and patronised by his wife. Then his intestines were removed and divided, the first set were given to the parish church in Saint-Germain-en-Laye and the others were presented to the Jesuit college, St Omer. His brain was also removed and stored in a lead casket and given to a Scots college based in Paris. Finally, the skin from his paralysed right arm was presented as relic to an order of English Augustine nuns also based in Paris.

What remained of the late king's corpse was placed in a lead-lined coffin and transported to the English Benedictine Abbey on Rue St Jacques, in Paris. Then the coffin rested in the Abbey chapel dedicated to St Edmund. The coffin was not interred because all concerned hoped that the late James's body would be repatriated to England and buried at Westminster Abbey. This was never to be the fate of the king's remains. Even after his daughter Anne ascended the throne that had once been her father's, James's remains continued to lie in Paris, but would not to remain in peace. His coffin was desecrated during the French Revolution. It is a sad and sacrilegious ending to a man who had known so little peace and tranquillity in his mortal life.

Those last years of his life in exile, if not James's happiest, I suspect may well have been his most content years – even if they were frustratingly littered with failed attempts to regain his lost thrones. This is especially true, I feel, after 1692, when he seems to have accepted his fate and to make the most of his remaining time through with religious devotion, visiting churches, reading and hunting, while being surrounded by like-minded people who supported him and believed in him. Those last six months of his life could not have been any more befitting if James had planned them himself. Falling ill on Good Friday, making a final royal progress on his pilgrimage to Bourbon, and being adored as a king en route, gave him an opportunity to mentally prepare for the end of his life in a semi-monastic and deeply devotional and meditative way, while dressing simply and taking water therapies. He was also able to mix with the local Capuchin monks. He died as he lived, devoted, stubborn, headstrong, determined and brave – never letting his convictions or faith fail him; in that way, he had achieved something his father had not, he died in his bed and at peace.

Conclusion

James II & VII was not born to be a king, he was that all important royal insurance policy: the royal spare. Although he did occupy the throne for not quite four years, he did not die a king; at least in no other capacity than through the maintenance of that title, twenty-three years after fleeing his kingdoms in late 1688.

Having examined the life experiences and events of King James II & VII, in the pages of this book, there is no one event that can be fully attributed to why James would become the last Catholic king of England and Britain, or why he was unable to maintain his position as king – it is a far more complex issue.

There are of course big factors that contribute to the fate of the displaced king, his religious conviction being the most obvious. As I have previously commented, James was, in my opinion, born a century and a half too late. His deep-held Catholic conviction, his firm belief in the idea of the divine right of kings, and his often pompous attitude, would have been better fitted to the sixteenth-century style of monarchy rather than a post–Reformation seventeenth-century king.

In today's secular and arguably enlightened age, the type of fevered religious devotion James expressed, especially after 1688, is generally incomprehensible to us today. This is especially so, as his faith and its very public pronouncement, would cost him so much both personally and politically. It is worth noting that to follow one's convictions, regardless of the possible outcomes and consequences – because let's face it, James was more than aware of what those potential and deadly consequences may have been – requires a great deal of personal courage and conviction. This is especially true when things do not unfold as expected. So, as much as there are many frustrating and less pleasant aspects to James's character, he should be admired for upholding and remaining devoted to his convictions and faith and being brave enough to live with their consequences.

To a degree it could be argued that his personal beliefs were not the biggest problem, but it was his unyielding personality and inability to keep his faith a private matter. Although he never went as far as the previous post–Reformation Catholic monarch, Mary Tudor – also known as Bloody Mary for her prosecution of Protestant subjects – James's personality left many fearing he could become just as tyrannical and 'bloody' as Mary had been. Had James been of a compromising nature, willing to keep his personal beliefs separate from state, to ensure any children with his second wife be raised Protestant – in a similar fashion to his eldest daughters from his marriage to Anne Hyde, the post-Restoration generation may well have been content to have him remain upon the throne regardless of personal convictions. Unfortunately, James was not of the same compromising nature as his elder brother, Charles II.

Events and personal experiences that contributed to these unyielding and stubborn personality traits within James's character can, with the help of hindsight, promote empathy towards this historical character who at times could be frustrating due to the decisions he made and their inevitable dramatic consequences. Of course, this also goes towards explaining why he would be the last Catholic king of Great Britain.

Given the childhood of the then prince and duke, who lived through the traumatic duration, and great political and social upheaval, of the Civil Wars, it is not surprising that these events may have helped form part of his character. Two of these traumatic events from his childhood include his father bringing him to witness battles and twice being taken captive and held for ransom. It is no wonder James had emotional and behaviour quirks that made him difficult and uncompromising, both as a man and as a king.

Some of his experiences as a child do seem to have affected how he viewed certain situations. He felt that his father's willingness to negotiate was a weakness. In contrast, during his years in his brother's Privy Council James is far more gung ho than other members – particularly concerning matters of military action and during the Anglo-Dutch wars. Part of this might have been due to the fact that the Dutch Republic were Protestant rather than Catholic, and also maybe his wanting to be active in his role as High Lord Admiral – but given others were far more cautious in wanting to take action, James was the exception rather than the majority.

Given the fate of his father and then the relative success of his brother, James must have felt an additional pressure to continue his brother's success and to succeed where his father failed. Unfortunately he did try to understand why one had failed and the other succeeded. For had he adopted a more flexible attitude, he would have been far more like his brother and less like his father.

Then there is the fact that James was the second son, a relationship-dynamic in ordinary non-royal families that can be problematic, both between siblings and between parent and child. Ideally James should never have been king, and seeing his brother being prepared as the heir – and given James's personality – there must have been jealousy at times. James also did not like his brother Charles acting in a parental way during their exile after the death of their father, leaving James to develop and exhibit an independent stubborn streak towards his brother. As the younger of the two siblings, James was emotionally less mature during that period than Charles, prone to tantrums and anger when he did not get what he wanted – a characteristic that never really resolved itself as he got older. Inability to resolve frustration and the desire to prove himself are both reasons that could explain why he never fully grew out of these traits.

The post-Restoration kingdoms inherited by James in February 1685 still had a collective memory of the Civil Wars of his father's reign, and of the grim interregnum years before the return of Charles II. In more recent years, thanks largely to the Exclusionist

Whig movement of the late 1670s, fear of Catholicism returned to the forefront of public political awareness.

Instead of using this knowledge and adjusting his attitude to alleviate fear and concern, James – whether intentionally in trying to prove his authority as king or not – presented to his subjects the autocratic, unforgiving tyrant that they, the Protestant majority, had always feared from a Catholic monarch. This was most evident in the aftermath of the Monmouth Rebellion less than six months into his new reign, and then again in the overly harsh Bloody Assizes after the rebellion was quashed. Although James had little alternative but to punish the leaders of the rebellion, and particularly his wayward nephew the Duke of Monmouth, he could have used this opportunity to demonstrate compassion towards the common folk caught up in the rebellion and show himself to be a just and forgiving king. Instead, James opted for the harshest of punishments to act as a deterrent; in so doing, he created an image of himself as a cruel tyrant and caused yet more harm to his reputation.

Another factor which contributed to James ultimately losing his thrones is the promotion of his fellow Catholics around him, something that was actually unlawful. This action demonstrates a lack of care or respect for the laws of the land, a tyrannical attitude to the population at large, and a disrespect for his Protestant courtiers.

This was made worse through his attempt to meddle with the Anglican church and how his subjects should pray. This is behaviour is trued of a convert to any faith, they feel their new faith is superior and so tend to be less tolerant of the views or beliefs of others; they also want to share their new feeling of spiritual contentment. Given his position as king and as the head of the Anglican communion, ruling over a majority of Protestant subjects, he needed to demonstrate more discretion, be more open minded and tolerant of other people's private views, as well as keeping his personal beliefs out of politics and the business of state. All these things James was unable or unwilling to do.

The breaking point came in 1688, when his previously safe and 'barren' queen gave birth to a Catholic male heir. This meant that

James was no longer a one off Catholic monarch. As he was in his fifties and previously had no male Catholic heirs, his subjects – though uncomfortable – could have tolerated him in what they expected to be a relatively short reign given. Things changed when there was the potential to reinstate a Catholic line and legacy of monarchs to rule a Protestant nation. Once again, James could have alleviated the problem if he had announced that his son would be brought up Protestant, just like his daughters Mary and Anne from his first marriage. However, James chose to interpret the birth of a healthy male heir as a sign that God was happy with him and he was on the right path to pleasing the almighty. He saw it as his moral duty to save the souls of his Protestant subjects and that his son would be able to continue his work after his eventual death. Although his intentions were not coming from a bad place, these thoughts and actions would inadvertently lose him his crown. He was blind to the fact that a Protestant society saw his notions as outdated.

At the time of the Glorious Revolution in 1688, we see James failing to grasp the problem and initially writing off the threat towards the kingdom and himself as trivial. This changed in the days and weeks following William of Orange's arrival in England and James's mental state deteriorated rapidly. He reverses decisions he had previously made, and was physically affected by the new stressful situation he was under. This stress materialised through repeated nose bleeds. In this state of panic and fear, he was in no way fit to fight for the thrones he was losing. Those who may have been able to help, him saw these physical weaknesses as a sign to change allegiance. One of these important people that James lost to the Williamite side was his top military commander and leader, John Churchill.

In the last years of his exile in France, when James attempted to get his thrones back, first in Ireland and then secondly off the coast of Normandy, he showed that he had lost his winning military flourish and accomplishments from his youth. He underestimated the experience and skill of his nephew and son-in-law, William. His reluctance to dismiss his men after the naval defeat in 1692, after the disastrous battles of Barfleur and La Hougue, indicates to me that he was mentally strong enough at this point to accept moving on and refuse on his son's Restoration rather than his own. The transformation of his life and focus after his return to Saint-Germain-en-Laye, changing into a reflective, pious and devout Catholic sees a man content for the first time in his adult life since being was a soldier for hire during his first exile with his brother Charles. During this time in James's life, when he was on his own personal and spiritual journey, he was, for the first time, allowed to reflect upon and accept all his experiences in life, the successes as well as what he perceived to be failings. Through his father he was able to turn this potentially frustrating and inactive period at the end of his life into a state of contentment and fulfilment. By adopting a devotional timetable and exploring this part of his life fully provided him with a daily routine and comfort when he needed it most.

James II & VII was the straw that broke the back English and British constitutional camel. Due to the Reformation under Henry VIII for England, and then the joint thrones of Scotland and England after 1603, the isle had struggled to resolve the social and political issue of the relationship and balance between church and state as well as Catholics and Protestants. Time and again, history before James was even born is littered with failed attempts to resolve the issue. But James's extreme religious opinions, his rashness and his inability to compromise were the perfect storm, at the perfect time to trigger the Glorious Revolution and bring forth a much-needed constitutional overhaul, settling this long-standing problem to this day. The biggest price he paid for inadvertently bringing stability was being the last Catholic king of England and Great Britain.

Bibliography

Primary

Historical Collections of Private Passages of State Volume 6, 1645–47 D. Browne London 1722

Hatton, Correspondence of the family of Hatton 1601–1704, (ed. Thompson E.M. 1878) Vol 1

The proceedings in the House of Commons, Touching on the Impeachment of Edward late Earl of Clarendon, Lord High Chancellor of England Anno 1667 (Egerton M.S. 3363 26 October – 18 December 1667)

Sir David Nairn, The life of a Scottish Jacobite at the Court of Exiled Stuarts, Peter Lang Ltd, 2018

Dalrymple, Sir John, *The Memoirs of Great Britain and Ireland from the Dissolution of the Last Parliament of Charles II Until the Sea Battle of La Hogue*, Volume III, W. Strahan, London, 1771

The Siege and History of Londonderry (ed.) Hempton John, Londonderry, 1861. (NB Dalrymple's account along with other primary sources about the siege are in this book)

Calendar of Manuscripts of the Dean and Chapter of Wells, Vol 2

Calendar of Manuscripts of the Marquess of Ormonde, new series Vol II

The Manuscripts of the most Honourable Marquis of Ormonde New series Vol 7

Register of the Privy Council of Scotland, Third Series Volume 11, 20 June 1685

Calendar of State Papers, Charles II Domestic series October 1683 – April 1684

Calendar of State Papers, Domestic, James II 1687–89

Echard, Laurence, *History of England, consisting of explanations and amendments, as well as new and curious additions to that History. Together with some Apologies and Vindications, by the same author*, London 1720

Evelyn, John, *The complete Diary of John Evelyn*, Everyman, 2006

The Register of the Privy Council of Scotland, Third Series, Volume 10; Edinburgh. HM General Register House.

Jesse, J.H. *Memories of the court of England during the reign of the Stuarts*, George Bell & sons, 1882.

London Gazette, Various dates

Morpeth, Lord Viscount Charles, Their papers about the affairs of Ireland, 1690

Memorandum, Anne Hyde, Duchess of York 1653–1671 MSS 15900BM (reprinted in a book 2018)

Pepys, Samuel, *The Diary of Samuel Pepys*, Penguin, 2003

Roberts, George, *The Life Progresses and Rebellion of James Duke of Monmouth to his capture and Execution: With an account of the Bloody Assize.* Vol 1 & 2, London, 1844

Story, George, *A true and impartial history of the most material occurrences in the Kingdom of Ireland during the two last years. With the present state of both armies. Written by an Eye-witness to the most remarkable passages*, London : For R. Chiswell, 1691.

Secondary

Brennan, Laura, *The Duke of Monmouth, Life and Rebellion*, Pen & Sword, 2018

Buchan, John, *The Nations of Today, A New History of the World, Ireland*, Hodder & Stoughton Limited, London, 1924.

Callow, John, *The making of King James II, The formative Years of a fallen King*, Sutton, 2000

Callow, John, *King in Exile , James II: Warrior King and Saint*, The History Press, 2004

Chandler, D., *Sedgemoor 1685: From Monmouth's invasion to the Bloody Assizes,* Staplehurst, Spellmount, 1995

Corp Edward, *Sir David Nairn, The life of a Scottish Jacobite at the Court of Exiled Stuarts*, Peter Lang ltd, 2018

Cruickshanks, Eveline, *The Glorious Revolution*, MacMillan Press, 2000

Doherty, Richard, *The Williamite war in Ireland 1688–1691*, Four Courts Press, 1998

Ede-Borrett, Stephen, *The Army of James II 1685-1688, The Birth of the British Army*, Helion, 2017

Fraser, Lady Antonia, *King Charles II*, Futura, 1979

Fraser, Lady Antonia, *Love and Louis XIV, The women in the life of the Sun King*, Orion, London, 2006

Glassey, L.K.J. *The reigns of Charles II and James II (Problems in focus)*, (Belgrave 1997)

Harris, Tim, *Restoration Charles II and his Kingdoms 1660–1685*, Penguin, 2005

Harris, Tim, *Revolution The Great Crisis of the British Monarchy 1685–1720*, Penguin 2006

Henslow, J.R. *Anne Hyde Duchess of York*, Forgotten books, 2018

Hill, Christopher, *Puritanism & Revolution*, Panther History, 1958

Horspool, David, *Cromwell*, Penguin Monarchs series, 2017

Greaves, Richard L. *Secrets of the Kingdom, British Radicals from the Popish Plot to the Revolution of 1688–89*, Stanford University Press, California, 1992

Jackson, Dr Clare, *Charles II*, Penguin Monarchs series 2018

Kishlansky, Mark, *A Monarchy Transformed – Britain 1603–1714*, Penguin, 1996

Luttrell, Narcissus, *A Brief Historical Relation of State Affairs: from September 1678 to April 1714*, volumes 1-6, University Press, Oxford 1974

Miller, John, *James II: A Study in Kingship*, Yale University Press 2000

Murray, R.H. *The Journal of John Stevens*, University of Oxford, London, 1912

Shepherd, Robert, *Ireland's Fate: The Boyne and after*, Aurum, London 1990

Spencer, Charles, *To Catch a King, Charles II's Great Escape*, Harper Colins UK, 2017

Stanier Clarke, James, *The life of James II of England Together with the king's advice to his son*, Arkose Press, 2015

Vallance, Edward, *The Glorious Revolution 1688 – Britain's Fight for Liberty*, Little Brown, 2006

Watson, J.N.P. *Captain, General and Rebel Chief: The life of James Duke of Monmouth*, George Allen & Unwin, 1979

Willock, John, *A Scots Earl in Covenanting Times: being life and times of Archibald 9th Earl of Argyll 1629–1685*, messenger publishing, 2007.

Womersley, David, *James II The Last Catholic King*, Penguin, 2019

Index